POEMS
1959·1975

POEMS
1959·1975

Yves Bonnefoy

A translation
by Richard Pevear
of *Pierre écrite* and
Dans le leurre du seuil

VINTAGE BOOKS
NEW YORK

FIRST VINTAGE BOOKS EDITION, June 1985

Parts of this translation originally appeared in *Paris Review,*
The New Yorker and *Translation.*

Library of Congress Cataloging in Publication Data

Bonnefoy, Yves.
Poems, 1959-1975.

English and French.
1. Bonnefoy, Yves—Translations, English.   I. Pevear,
Richard, 1943-   .   II. Bonnefoy, Yves.   Dans le
leurre du seuil.   English & French.   1985.   III. Title.
[PQ2603.0533A26   1985b]   841'.914   84-25778
ISBN 0-394-73956-6 (pbk.)

Manufactured in the United States of America

2 4 6 8 9 7 5 3

A Note on the Translations

These translations are as faithful to the originals as I have been able
to make them. The meaning and truth of speech being problematical
anyway, I have had the additional problem of finding English equivalents of the words *sens*, *vrai* and *parole*, which speak for central
concerns in Yves Bonnefoy's poetry, and which do not quite mean
"meaning," "true" and "speech." Though I have taken no liberties, I
have allowed myself a certain freedom, sometimes at the poet's urging
(he kindly read through two versions and offered many clarifications).
So, for instance, where he refers to *le vrai jardin*, I have put simply
"the garden."

Bonnefoy is the poet of that garden. He sometimes takes the serpent's part, as poets will. The translator's part is similar, in a narrower
sense.

—Richard Pevear

Contents

WRITTEN STONE (1965)

THE LURE OF THE THRESHOLD (1975)

POEMS
1959·1975

WRITTEN STONE

Pierre écrite

1965

"Thou mettest with things dying;
I with things new-born."

—THE WINTER'S TALE

L'été de nuit

L'ÉTÉ DE NUIT

I

Il me semble, ce soir,
Que le ciel étoilé, s'élargissant,
Se rapproche de nous; et que la nuit,
Derrière tant de fleux, est moins obscure.

Et le feuillage aussi brille sous le feuillage,
Le vert, et l'orangé des fruits mûrs, s'est accru,
Lampe d'un ange proche; un battement
De lumière cachée prend l'arbre universel.

Il me semble, ce soir,
Que nous sommes entrés dans le jardin, dont l'ange
A refermé les portes sans retour.

II

Navire d'un été,
Et toi comme à la proue, comme le temps s'achève,
Dépliant des étoffes peintes, parlant bas.

Dans ce rêve de mai,
L'éternité montait parmi les fruits de l'arbre

THE SUMMER'S NIGHT

I

It seems to me that the starry sky
Is swelling tonight, is drawing
Closer to us; and the dark,
Behind so many fires, is less obscure.

And the leaves, too, are shining under the leaves,
The green, and the orange of ripe fruit has deepened,
Lamp of a nearby angel; a flutter
Of hidden light runs through the universal tree.

It seems to me, tonight,
That we have come into the garden whose gates
The angel shut behind us forever.

II

The ship of one summer, and you
As if at the bow, in the fullness of time,
Unfolding painted cloths, talking softly.

In this May dream,
Eternity rose among the fruits of the tree,

3

Et je t'offrais le fruit qui illimite l'arbre
Sans angoisse ni mort, d'un monde partagé.

Vaguent au loin les morts au désert de l'écume,
Il n'est plus de désert puisque tout est en nous
Et il n'est plus de mort puisque mes lèvres touchent
L'eau d'une ressemblance éparse sur la mer.

O suffisance de l'été, je t'avais pure
Comme l'eau qu'a changée l'étoile, comme un bruit
D'écume sous nos pas d'où la blancheur du sable
Remonte pour bénir nos corps inéclairés.

III

Le mouvement
Nous était apparu la faute, et nous allions
Dans l'immobilité comme sous le navire
Bouge et ne bouge pas le feuillage des morts.

Je te disais ma figure de proue
Heureuse, indifférente, qui conduit,
Les yeux à demi-clos, le navire de vivre
Et rêve comme il rêve, étant sa paix profonde,
Et s'arque sur l'étrave où bat l'antique amour.

Souriante, première, délavée,
A jamais le reflet d'une étoile immobile
Dans le geste mortel.
Aimée, dans le feuillage de la mer.

IV

Terre comme gréée,
Vois,
C'est ta figure de proue,
Tachée de rouge.

And I offered you the fruit that unbinds the tree,
A shared world, with no anguish or death.

Far off the dead wander in the desert of foam,
No more a desert since all is within us
And no more death since my lips touch
The water of a likeness scattered on the sea.

O bounty of summer, I had you pure
As water changed by the star, as the sound
Of surf under our footsteps where the sand's whiteness
Shines back to bless our unlit bodies.

III

Movement
Had seemed a sin to us, so we went
Into stillness as the leaves of the dead
Stir and do not stir under the ship.

I called you my figure at the prow,
Happy, indifferent, who with half-closed eyes
Guide the ship of living
And dream as it dreams, being its deep peace,
Arched over the bow where love has always pulsed.

Smiling, wave-washed, primal,
Forever the shining of a motionless star
In the mortal gesture.
Beloved, in the long leaves of the sea.

IV

Earth as if rigged
For the wind,
This is the figure,
Red-stained, at your prow.

L'étoile, l'eau, le sommeil
Ont usé cette épaule nue
Qui a frémi puis se penche
A l'Orient où glace le cœur.

L'huile méditante a régné
Sur son corps aux ombres qui bougent,
Et pourtant elle ploie sa nuque
Comme on pèse l'âme des morts.

V

Voici presque l'instant
Où il n'est plus de jour, plus de unit, tant l'étoile
A grandi pour bénir ce corps brun, souriant,
Illimité, une eau qui sans chimère bouge.

Ces frêles mains terrestres dénoueront
Le nœud triste des rêves.
La clarté protégée reposera
Sur la table des eaux.

L'étoile aime l'écume, et brûlera
Dans cette robe grise.

. . . VI

Longtemps ce fut l'été. Une étoile immobile
Dominait les soleils tournants. L'été de nuit
Portait l'été de jour dans ses mains de lumière
Et nous nous parlions bas, en feuillage de nuit.

L'étoile indifférente; et l'étrave; et le clair
Chemin de l'une à l'autre en eaux et ciels tranquilles.
Tout ce qui est bougeait comme un vaisseau qui tourne
Et glisse, et ne sait plus son âme dans la nuit.

Star, water, and sleep
Have worn her bare shoulder
Which shivered and now turns
East where the heart freezes.

Meditative oil ruled
Her body in the moving shadows,
Yet she bends her neck
As souls of the dead are weighed.

V

It is nearly the hour
When day and night are no more, so great
Has the star grown to bless this brown body, smiling,
Limitless, water stirred by no chimera.

These fragile earthly hands will undo
The sad knot of dreams.
The shielded light will rest
On the table of the waters.

The star loves the foam,
And will burn in that gray dress.

. . . VI

For long it was summer. A motionless star
Overruled the turning suns. The summer's night
Bore the summer's day in its shining hands
And we talked together softly, in the leaves of night.

Indifferent star; ship's bow; and the bright path
From one to the other in quiet skies and seas.
Like a vessel turning, slipping, all that is
Moved, and no longer knew its soul in the night.

VII

N'avions-nous pas l'été à franchir, comme un large
Océan immobile, et moi simple, couché
Sur les yeux et la bouche et l'âme de l'étrave,
Aimant l'été, buvant tes yeux sans souvenirs,

N'étais-je pas le rêve aux prunelles absentes
Qui prend et ne prend pas, et ne veut retenir
De ta couleur d'été qu'un bleu d'une autre pierre
Pour un été plus grand, où rien ne peut finir?

VIII

Mais ton épaule se déchire dans les arbres,
Ciel étoilé, et ta bouche recherche
Les fleuves respirants de la terre pour vivre
Parmi nous ta soucieuse et désirante nuit.

O notre image encor,
Tu portes près du cœur une même blessure,
Une même lumière où bouge un même fer.

Divise-toi, qui es l'absence et ses marées.
Accueille-nous, qui avons goût de fruits qui tombent,
Mêle-nous sur tes plages vides dans l'écume
Avec les bois d'épave de la mort,

Arbre aux rameaux de nuit doubles, doubles toujours.

IX

Eaux du dormeur, arbre d'absence, heures sans rives,
Dans votre éternité une nuit va finir.
Comment nommerons-nous cet autre jour, mon âme,
Ce plus bas rougeoiement mêlé de sable noir?

Dans les eaux du dormeur les lumières se troublent.
Un langage se fait, qui partage le clair
Buissonnement d'étoiles dans l'écume.
Et c'est presque l'éveil, déjà le souvenir.

8

VII

Didn't we have summer to cross, like a wide
Still ocean, and I lying
On the eyes, the mouth, the soul of the ship's bow,
Loving summer, drinking your unmemoried eyes,

Wasn't I the vacant-eyed dream
That takes and does not take, and wants to keep
Of your summer color only a more intense blue,
Stone for a summer, where nothing would end?

VIII

But your shoulder is torn among the trees,
Starry sky, and your mouth seeks
The breathing rivers of the earth to live
Through your anxious, yearning night among us.

O still our image,
You bear the same wound near your heart,
The same light where the same iron stirs.

Divide yourself, who are absence and its tides.
Receive us, who have the taste of fallen fruit,
Mingle us in the foam of your empty beaches
With the driftwood of death, tree

Of the doubling, the ever-doubling branches of night.

IX

Waters of the sleeper, tree of absence, shoreless hours,
In your eternity a night is ending.
How shall we name this new day, my soul,
This gentle glowing mixed with blacker sand?

In the waters of the sleeper the lights grow dim.
A language begins to form, which parts
The bright burgeoning of stars in the foam.
Awakening is near, and with it memory.

UNE PIERRE

« Regarde-moi
Là-bas, dans cet espace que transit
Une eau rapide et noire . . . »

Je t'inventais
Sous l'arche d'un miroir orageux, qui prenait
La parcelle d'un rouge en toi, impartageable,
Et l'enflammait « là-bas », au mascaret de mort.

LE JARDIN

Les étoiles voûtaient les murs du haut jardin
Comme les fruits de l'arbre au-delà, mais les pierres
Du lieu mortel portaient dans l'écume de l'arbre
Comme une ombre d'étrave et comme un souvenir.

Étoiles et vous, craies d'un pur chemin,
Vous pâlissiez, vous nous preniez le vrai jardin,
Tous les chemins du ciel étoilé faisant ombre
Sur ce chant naufragé; sur notre route obscure.

Dans ses coffres le rêve a replié

Dans ses coffres le rêve a replié
Ses étoffes peintes, et l'ombre
De ce visage taché
De l'argile rouge des morts.

Tu n'as pas voulu retenir
Ces mains étroites qui firent
Le signe de solitude
Sur les pentes ocres d'un corps.

A STONE

"Look at me
There, in that space chilled
By a swift, dark stream . . ."

Under the arch
Of a stormy mirror I invented you, who took
A bit of the indivisible redness that you are
And set fire to it "there," in the flood-tide of death.

THE GARDEN

The stars hung over the walls of the high garden
Like fruit on a tree beyond, but the stones
Of the mortal place bore through the foam of the tree,
The shadow of a ship's bow, of a memory.

Stars, chalks of a pure road,
You faded, you took the garden from us,
And all roads of the sky grew dark
Over this shipwrecked song; over our obscure way.

In its chests the dream has folded

In its chests the dream has folded
Its painted cloths away,
And the shadow of this face stained
With the red clay of the dead.

You did not want to keep
These narrow hands that made
The sign of solitude
Over the ochre slopes of a body.

Et telle une eau qui se perd
Dans les rougeurs d'une eau sombre,
La nuque proche se courbe
Sur la plage où brille la mort.

L'ÉCUME, LE RÉCIF

Solitude à ne pas gravir, que de chemins!
Robe rouge, que d'heures proches sous les arbres!
Mais adieu, dans cette aube froide, mon eau pure,
Adieu malgré le cri, l'épaule, le sommeil.

Écoute, il ne faut plus ces mains qui se reprennent
Comme éternellement l'écume et le rocher,
Et même plus ces yeux qui se tournent vers l'ombre,
Aimant mieux le sommeil encore partagé.

Il ne faut plus tenter d'unir voix et prière,
Espoir et nuit, désirs de l'abîme et du port.
Vois, ce n'est pas Mozart qui lutte dans ton âme,
Mais le gong, contre l'arme informe de la mort.

Adieu, visage en mai.
Le bleu du ciel est morne aujourd'hui, ici.
Le glaive de l'indifférence de l'étoile
Blesse une fois de plus la terre du dormeur.

LA LAMPE, LE DORMEUR

I

Je ne savais dormir sans toi, je n'osais pas
Risquer sans toi les marches descendantes.
Plus tard, j'ai découvert que c'est un autre songe,
Cette terre aux chemins qui tombent dans la mort.

And like water sinking
Into the blushes of dark waves,
The near neck bends
Over the beach where death shines.

THE FOAM, THE REEF

Unscalable solitude, and so many paths!
Red dress, so many hours for us under the trees!
But farewell, in this cold dawn, my pure water,
Farewell despite the cry, the shoulder, the sleep.

Listen, we have no more need of these hands
That clutch each other as foam and rock do, eternally,
Nor even of these eyes that turn toward darkness,
Preferring sleep because it is still shared.

We must not keep trying to join voice and prayer,
Hope and night, longing for the deeps and the port.
You see, it is not Mozart fighting in your soul
But a gong, against the formless weapon of death.

Farewell, face in the light of May.
The blue sky is cheerless here, today.
Again the sword of the star's indifference
Wounds the sleeper's earth.

THE LAMP, THE SLEEPER

I

I did not know how to sleep without you,
Did not dare risk the descending steps without you.
Later, I learned that this earth, whose paths
Fall into death, is another dream.

13

Alors je t'ai voulue au chevet de ma fièvre
D'inexister, d'être plus noir que tant de nuit,
Et quand je parlais haut dans le monde inutile,
Je t'avais sur les voies de trop vaste sommeil.

Le dieu pressant en moi, c'étaient ces rives
Que j'éclairais de l'huile errante, et tu sauvais
Nuit après nuit mes pas du gouffre qui m'obsède,
Nuit après nuit mon aube, inachevable amour.

II

— Je me penchais sur toi, vallée de tant de pierres,
J'écoutais les rumeurs de ton grave repos,
J'apercevais très bas dans l'ombre qui te couvre
Le lieu triste où blanchit l'écume du sommeil.

Je t'écoutais rêver. O monotone et sourde,
Et parfois par un roc invisible brisée,
Comme ta voix s'en va, ouvrant parmi ses ombres
Le gave d'une étroite attente murmurée!

Là-haut, dans les jardins de l'émail, il est vrai
Qu'un paon impie s'accroît des lumières mortelles.
Mais toi il te suffit de ma flamme qui bouge,
Tu habites la nuit d'une phrase courbée.

Qui es-tu? Je ne sais de toi que les alarmes,
Les hâtes dans ta voix d'un rite inachevé.
Tu partages l'obscur au sommet de la table,
Et que tes mains sont nues, ô seules éclairées!

Bouche, tu auras bu

Bouche, tu auras bu
A la saveur obscure,
A une eau ensablée,
A l'Être sans retour.

14

Then I wanted you at the bedside of my fever
Of not existing, of being blacker than such night,
And when I spoke aloud in the useless world,
I kept you with me on the vast ways of sleep.

The urgent god within me was these banks
Which I lit with vagrant oil, and you saved
My steps night after night from the pit that haunts me,
Night after night my dawn, unattainable love.

II

—I bent above you, valley full of stones,
I listened to the murmurs of your grave repose.
I could see far down in the darkness that covers you
The sad place where sleep's white foam glimmers.

I listened to you dreaming. O monotonous and hollow,
And sometimes broken by an unseen rock,
How your voice goes on, opening among its shadows
The narrow stream of a long-whispered hope.

Up there, it's true, in enamel's gardens,
An impious peacock feeds on mortal lights.
But for you my shifting flame is enough,
You dwell in the night of a vaulted phrase.

Who are you? I only know your sudden fears,
The urgings of an uncompleted rite in your voice.
You divide the darkness at the summit of the table,
And how bare your hands are, alone in my light!

Mouth, you will have drunk

Mouth, you will have drunk
Of the dark savor,
Of silted water,
Of Being without return.

Où vont se réunir
L'eau amère, l'eau douce,
Tu auras bu où brille
L'impartageable amour.

Mais ne t'angoisse pas,
O bouche qui demandes
Plus qu'un reflet troublé,
Plus qu'une ombre de jour :

L'âme se fait d'aimer
L'écume sans réponse.
La joie sauve la joie,
L'amour le non-amour.

UNE PIERRE

Il me disait, Tu es une eau, la plus obscure,
La plus fraîche où goûter l'impartageable amour.
J'ai retenu son pas, mais parmi d'autres pierres,
Dans le boire éternel du jour plus bas que jour.

Where the bitter water
Mingles with the sweet,
You will have drunk
Where unshareable love shines.

But do not be distressed,
O mouth that asks
For more than dim reflections,
More than shadows of day.

The soul is made by loving
The unresponding foam.
Joy gives life to joy,
Love saves what is not love.

A STONE

He said to me, You are water, the darkest,
The coolest bearing the taste of unshareable love.
I kept his footstep, but among other stones,
In the eternal drinking of day beneath the light of day.

Pierre écrite

Prestige, disais-tu

Prestige, disais-tu, de notre lampe et des feuillages,
Ces hôtes de nos soirs.
Ils tirent jusqu'à nous leurs barques sur les dalles,
Ils connaissent notre désir de l'éternel.

La nuit parfaite dans le ciel criant son feu,
Eux sont venus d'un pas sans ombre, ils nous éveillent,
Leur parole commence au tremblé de nos voix.

Le pas des astres mesurant le sol dallé de cette nuit,
Et ceux mêlant à tant de feux l'obscurité propre de l'homme.

UNE PIERRE

Il désirait, sans connaître,
Il a péri, sans avoir.
Arbres, fumées,
Toutes lignes de vent et de déception
Furent son gîte.
Infiniment
Il n'a étreint que sa mort.

Written Stone

The spell, you said

The spell, you said, of our lamp and the leaves,
These guests of our evenings.
They draw their boats up to us on the flags,
They know our thirst for the eternal.

While perfect night cries its fire overhead,
They come with shadowless steps and wake us,
Their speech begins at the tremor of our voices.

Stars pace out the paved ground of the night,
But they add a human darkness to so many fires.

A STONE

He desired without knowing,
He died without having.
Trees, mists,
All lines of the wind and disappointment
Were his refuge.
He embraced
Nothing infinitely but his death.

LE LIEU DES MORTS

Quel est le lieu des morts,
Ont-ils droit comme nous à des chemins,
Parlent-ils, plus réels étant leurs mots,
Sont-ils l'esprit des feuillages ou des feuillages plus hauts?

Phénix a-t-il construit pour eux un château,
Dressé pour eux une table?
Le cri de quelque oiseau dans le feu de quelque arbre
Est-il l'espace où ils se pressent tous?

Peut-être gisent-ils dans la feuille du lierre,
Leur parole défaite
Étant le port de la déchirure des feuilles, où la nuit vient.

UNE PIERRE

Je fus assez belle.
Il se peut qu'un jour comme celui-ci me ressemble
Mais la ronce l'emporte sur mon visage,
La pierre accable mon corps.

Approche-toi,
Servante verticale rayée de noir,
Et ton visage court.

Répands le lait ténébreux, qui exalte
Ma force simple.
Sois-moi fidèle,
Nourrice encor, mais d'immortalité.

THE PLACE OF THE DEAD

What is the place of the dead,
Do they have a right to move about as we do,
Do they speak, are their words more real,
Are they the spirit of the leaves, or higher leaves?

Has Phoenix built a castle for them
Or set them a table?
Is the call of a bird in the fire of a tree
The space they all crowd into?

Perhaps they rest in a leaf of ivy,
Their unmade speech
The port of the rent in the leaves, where night comes.

A STONE

I was quite beautiful.
A day like this might resemble me.
But the thornbush triumphs over my face,
The stone weighs down my body.

Bend to me,
My vertical servant striped in black,
With your short face.

Pour out the shadowy milk that exalts
My simple strength.
Be faithful to me,
Still my nurse, but in immortality.

LE LIEU DES MORTS

Le lieu des morts,
C'est peut-être le pli de l'étoffe rouge.
Peut-être tombent-ils
Dans ses mains rocailleuses; s'aggravent-ils
Dans les touffes en mer de la couleur rouge;
Ont-ils comme miroir
Le corps gris de la jeune aveugle; ont-ils pour faim
Dans le chant des oiseaux ses mains de noyée.

Ou sont-ils réunis sous le sycomore ou l'érable?
Nul bruit ne trouble plus leur assemblée.
La déesse se tient au sommet de l'arbre,
Elle incline vers eux l'aiguière d'or.

Et seul parfois le bras divin brille dans l'arbre
Et des oiseaux se taisent, d'autres oiseaux.

UNE PIERRE

Deux ans, ou trois,
Je me sentis suffisante. Les astres,
Les fleuves, les forêts ne m'égalaient pas.
La lune s'écaillait sur mes robes grises.
Mes yeux cernés
Illuminaient les mers sous leurs voûtes d'ombre,
Et mes cheveux étaient plus amples que ce monde
Aux yeux vaincus, aux cris qui ne m'atteignaient pas.

Des bêtes de nuit hurlent, c'est mon chemin,
Des portes noires se ferment.

THE PLACE OF THE DEAD

The place of the dead
May be a fold in red cloth.
They may fall
Into its rough hands; deepen
In sea-borne tufts of the color red;
Have for a mirror
The gray body of a blind girl; for hunger
In the song of birds a drowned girl's hands.

Or have they met under sycamore or maple?
No noise disturbs their gathering now.
The goddess stands at the summit of the tree,
She tips the golden pitcher toward them.

Sometimes only the divine arm gleams in the tree
And the birds, other birds, fall silent.

A STONE

For two or three years
I was pleased with myself. Stars,
Rivers, forests, could not compare with me.
The moon sifted down on my gray robes.
From their dark arches
My deep-set eyes lit up the seas,
And my hair was more abundant than this world
With its downcast look, its cries that could not reach me.

Night creatures howl, this is my path now,
Black doors shut.

UNE PIERRE

Ta jambe, nuit très dense,
Tes seins, liés,
Si noirs, ai-je perdu mes yeux,
Mes nerfs d'atroce vue
Dans cette obscurité plus âpre que la pierre,
O mon amour?

Au centre de la lumière, j'abolis
D'abord ma tête crevassée par le gaz,
Mon nom ensuite avec tous pays,
Mes mains seules droites persistent.

En tête de cortège je suis tombé
Sans dieu, sans voix audible, sans péché,
Bête trinitaire criante.

UNE PIERRE

Tombe, mais douce pluie, sur le visage.
Éteins, mais lentement, le très pauvre chaleil.

JEAN ET JEANNE

Tu demandes le nom
De cette maison basse délabrée,
C'est Jean et Jeanne en un autre pays.

Quand les larges vents passent
Le seuil où rien ne chante ni paraît.

C'est Jean et Jeanne et de leurs faces grises
Le plâtre du jour tombe et je revois
La vitre des étés anciens. Te souviens-tu?
La plus brillante au loin, l'arche fille des ombres.

A STONE

Your leg, deepest night,
Your breasts, bound,
So black, have I lost my eyes,
My nerves of agonized seeing
In this darkness harsher than stone,
O my love?

At the center of light, I abolish
First my head cracked by gas,
Then my name with all lands,
Only my straight hands persist.

At the head of the procession
I have fallen, godless, voiceless, sinless,
A crying trinitarian beast.

A STONE

Fall but gently, rain, upon this face.
Put out, but slowly, this humble cresset lamp.

JOHN AND JOAN

You ask the name
Of this low, decaying house,
It is John and Joan in another country.

When the wide winds cross
The threshold where nothing sings or shows.

It is John and Joan and the plaster of day
Falls from their gray faces and I see again
The window of long past summers. Do you remember?
Brightest in the distance, the arch, child of shadows.

Aujourd'hui, ce soir, nous ferons un feu
Dans la grande salle.
Nous nous éloignerons,
Nous le laisserons vivre pour les morts.

UNE PIERRE

Aglaure s'est dressée
Dans les feuilles mortes.
Sa taille enfiévrée s'est reformée
Sous des mains diligentes.
Sa nuque s'est ployée sous la chaleur des lèvres.
La nuit vint, qui couvrit sa face dévastée
Et ses sanglots épars dans le lit de la glaise.

UNE PIERRE

Longtemps dura l'enfance au mur sombre et je fus
La conscience d'hiver; qui se pencha
Tristement, fortement, sur une image,
Amèrement, sur le reflet d'un autre jour.

N'ayant rien désiré
Plus que de contribuer à mêler deux lumières,
O mémoire, je fus
Dans son vaisseau de verre l'huile diurne
Criant son âme rouge au ciel des longues pluies.

Qu'aurai-je aimé? L'écume de la mer
Au-dessus de Trieste, quand le gris
De la mer de Trieste éblouissait
Les yeux du sphinx déchirable des rives.

Today, tonight, we will light a fire
In the big room,
Withdraw
And leave it to live for the dead.

A STONE

Aglaura stands
Among the dead leaves.
Her feverish waist has been reshaped
By urgent hands,
Her neck bent under the heat of lips.
Night comes, covering her ravaged face
And her sobs scattered over the bed of clay.

A STONE

Childhood was long by the grim wall and I was
The mind of winter, bending
Sadly, stubbornly, over an image,
Bitterly, over the reflection of another day.

Having desired nothing
So much as to help in the blending of two lights,
O memory, I was
Diurnal oil in its glass vessel
Crying its red soul to the long rains of the sky.

What will I have loved? The sea's foam
Above Trieste, when the gray
Of the sea of Trieste dazzled
The eyes of the erodible sphinx of the shores.

UNE PIERRE

Orages puis orages je ne fus
Qu'un chemin de la terre.
Mais les pluies apaisaient l'inapaisable terre,
Mourir a fait le lit de la nuit dans mon cœur.

UNE PIERRE

Le livre de Porphyre sur le soleil,
Regarde-le tel qu'un amas de pierres noires.
J'ai lu longtemps le livre de Porphyre,
Je suis venu au lieu de nul soleil.

UNE PIERRE

O dite à demi-voix parmi les branches,
O murmurée, ô tue,
Porteuse d'éternel, lune, entrouvre les grilles
Et penche-toi pour nous qui n'avons plus de jour.

La face la plus sombre

La face la plus sombre a crié
Que le jour est proche.
En vain le buis s'est-il resserré
Sur le vieux jardin.

Ce peuple aussi a sa plainte,
Cette absence, son espoir.
Mais la lune se couvre et l'ombre
Emplit la bouche des morts.

A STONE

Storm after storm I was only
A path on the earth.
But the rains appeased the unappeasable earth,
Dying has made night's bed where my heart was.

A STONE

Take Porphyry's treatise on the sun
As no more than a heap of black stones.
After years of studying Porphyry's treatise,
I have come to a sunless place.

A STONE

O half-whispered among the branches,
O murmured, o hushed,
Bearer of the eternal, moon, slip through the gates,
Bend down to us who have no more day.

The darkest face

The darkest face has cried out
That day is near.
In vain has the hedge closed
Around the old garden.

This people too has its complaint,
This absence, its hope.
But the moon is hidden now and darkness
Fills the mouths of the dead.

SUR UN ÉROS DE BRONZE

Tu vieillissais dans les plis
De la grisaille divine.
Qui est venu, d'une lampe,
Empourprer ton horizon nu?

L'enfant sans hâte ni bruit
T'a découvert une route.
— Ce n'est pas que l'antique nuit
En toi ne s'angoisse plus.

Le même enfant volant bas
Dans la ténèbre des voûtes
A saisi ce cœur et l'emporte
Dans le feuillage inconnu.

UNE VOIX

Nous vieillissions, lui le feuillage et moi la source,
Lui le peu de soleil et moi la profondeur,
Et lui la mort et moi la sagesse de vivre.

J'acceptais que le temps nous présentât dans l'ombre
Son visage de faune au rire non moqueur,
J'aimais que se levât le vent qui porte l'ombre

Et que mourir ne fût en obscure fontaine
Que troubler l'eau sans fond que le lierre buvait.
J'aimais, j'étais debout dans le songe éternel.

ON A BRONZE EROS

You grew old in the folds
Of the holy grisaille.
Who has come, with a lamp,
To color your bare horizon?

Quiet, unhurried, the child
Has found you a way.
—Not that ancient night
Does not suffer in you still.

The same child flying down
Through the shade of the vaults
Has seized this heart and bears it
Away into unknown trees.

A VOICE

We grew old, he the leaves and I the pool,
He a patch of sunlight and I the depths,
He death and I the wisdom that chose life.

I consented that time would show us in the dark
His faun's face with its unmocking laugh,
I was glad that the dark-bearing wind would rise

And that dying was but a slight troubling
Of the fathomless water where the ivy drank.
I was glad, I stood in the eternal dream.

Un feu va devant nous

LA CHAMBRE

Le miroir et le fleuve en crue, ce matin,
S'appelaient à travers la chambre, deux lumières
Se trouvent et s'unissent dans l'obscur
Des meubles de la chambre descellée.

Et nous étions deux pays de sommeil
Communiquant par leurs marches de pierre
Où se perdait l'eau non trouble d'un rêve,
Toujours se reformant, toujours brisé.

La main pure dormait près de la main soucieuse.
Un corps un peu parfois dans son rêve bougeait.
Et loin, sur l'eau plus noire d'une table,
La robe rouge éclairante dormait.

L'ÉPAULE

Ton épaule soit l'aube, ayant porté
Tout mon obscur déchirement de nuit
Et toute cette écume amère des images,
Tout ce haut rougeoiement d'un impossible été.

A Fire Goes Before Us

THE ROOM

Mirror and flooding stream
Called to each other across the room this morning,
Two lights meet and join in the furnished
Darkness of the unsealed room.

And we were two countries of sleep
Connected by a flight of stone steps
Where the unclouded water of a dream ran down,
Forever recollecting and forever broken.

The pure hand slept beside the anxious hand.
Sometimes a body stirred lightly in its dreaming.
And away on the blacker water of a table
Slept the red, illuminating dress.

THE SHOULDER

Let your shoulder be the dawn, for it has borne
All my dark harrowing by night
And all this bitter foam of images,
This high glowing of an impossible summer.

Ton corps voûte pour nous son heure respirante
Comme un pays plus clair sur nos ombres penché
— Longue soit la journée où glisse, miroitante,
L'eau d'un rêve à l'afflux rapide, irrévélé.

O dans le bruissement du feuillage de l'arbre
Soit le masque aux yeux clos du rêve déposé!
J'entends déjà grandir le bruit d'un autre gave
Qui s'apaise, ou se perd, dans notre éternité.

L'ARBRE, LA LAMPE

L'arbre vieillit dans l'arbre, c'est l'été.
L'oiseau franchit le chant de l'oiseau et s'évade.
Le rouge de la robe illumine et disperse
Loin, au ciel, le charroi de l'antique douleur.

O fragile pays,
Comme la flamme d'une lampe que l'on porte,
Proche étant le sommeil dans la sève du monde,
Simple le battement de l'âme partagée.

Toi aussi tu aimes l'instant où la lumière des lampes
Se décolore et rêve dans le jour.
Tu sais que c'est l'obscur de ton cœur qui guérit,
La barque qui rejoint le rivage en tombe.

LES CHEMINS

Chemins, parmi
La matière des arbres. Dieux, parmi
Les touffes de ce chant inlassable d'oiseaux.
Et tout ton sang voûté sous une main rêveuse,
O proche, ô tout mon jour.

Let your body arch its breathing hour for us
Like a brighter country bent above our shadows
—Long be the day when the water of dreams
Runs shimmering, a quick flow, undisclosed.

O in the rustling leaves of the tree
Let the closed-eyed mask of the dream be hung!
Now I hear the sound of another stream rising,
To be stilled, or lost, in our eternity.

THE TREE, THE LAMP

The tree grows old in the tree, it is summer.
The bird leaps beyond birdsong and is gone.
The red of the dress illuminates and scatters
Away, in the sky, the lading of old sorrow.

O fragile country,
Like the flame of a lamp carried out-of-doors,
Sleep being close in the world's sap,
Simple the beating of the shared soul.

You too love the moment when the light of lamps
Fades and dreams into daylight.
You know it's the darkness of your own heart healing,
The boat that reaches shore and falls.

THE PATHS

Paths among
The matter of trees. Gods among
The tufts of this tireless song of birds.
And all your blood bent under a dreaming hand,
O near one, O my whole day.

Qui ramassa le fer
Rouillé, parmi les hautes herbes, n'oublie plus
Qu'aux grumeaux du métal la lumière peut prendre
Et consumer le sel du doute et de la mort.

LE MYRTE

Parfois je te savais la terre, je buvais
Sur tes lèvres l'angoisse des fontaines
Quand elle sourd des pierres chaudes, et l'été
Dominait haut la pierre heureuse et buveur.

Parfois je te disais de myrte et nous brûlions
L'arbre de tous tes gestes tout un jour.
C'étaient de grands feux brefs de lumière vestale,
Ainsi je t'inventais parmi tes cheveux clairs.

Tout un grand été nul avait séché nos rêves,
Rouillé nos voix, accru nos corps, défait nos fers.
Parfois le lit tournait comme une barque libre
Qui gagne lentement le plus haut de la mer.

LE SANG, LA NOTE SI

Longues, longues journées.
Le sang inapaisé heurte le sang.
Le nageur est aveugle.
Il descend par étages pourpres dans le battement de ton cœur.

Quand la nuque se tend
Le cri toujours désert prend une bouche pure.

Ainsi vieillit l'été. Ainsi la mort
Encercle le bonheur de la flamme qui bouge.
Et nous dormons un peu. La note si
Résonne très longtemps dans l'étoffe rouge.

He who gathered rusted
Iron among the high grasses, will not
Forget that in lumps of metal light can catch
And consume the salt of doubt and death.

﹡

MYRTLE

I knew you sometimes as the earth,
From your lips I drank the anguish of springs
As it wells up from sun-warmed stones, and high summer
Looked down on the blessed stone and the drinker.

Sometimes I said you were myrtle and we burned
The tree of all your gestures for a day.
They were high, brief fires of vestal light,
Thus I invented you amidst your bright hair.

One long empty summer dried up our dreams,
Rusted our voices, increased our bodies, loosed our chains.
The bed turned sometimes like an unmoored boat
That slowly makes its way to the open sea.

BLOOD, THE NOTE B

Long, long days.
Blood hurls against blood, unappeased.
The swimmer is blind.
He drops by crimson stages into the beating of your heart.

When the neck is tensed
The always empty cry comes to a pure mouth.

So summer grows old. So death
Surrounds the gladness of a dancing flame.
And we sleep a little. The note B
Echoes for a long time in the red cloth.

L'ABEILLE, LA COULEUR

Cinq heures.
Le sommeil est léger, en taches sur les vitres.
Le jour puise là-bas dans la couleur l'eau fraîche,
Ruisselante, du soir.

Et c'est comme si l'âme se simplifie
Étant lumière davantage, et qui rassure,
Mais, l'Un se déchirant contre la jambe obscure,
Tu te perds, où la bouche a bu à l'âcre mort.

(La corne d'abondance avec le fruit
Rouge dans le soleil qui tourne. Et tout ce bruit
D'abeilles de l'impure et douce éternité
Sur le si proche pré si brûlant encore).

LE SOIR

Rayures bleues et noires.
Un labour qui dévie vers le bas du ciel.
Le lit, vaste et brisé comme le fleuve en crue.
— Vois, c'est déjà le soir,
Et le feu parle auprès de nous dans l'éternité de la sauge.

LA LUMIÈRE DU SOIR

Le soir,
Ces oiseaux qui se parlent, indéfinis,
Qui se mordent, lumière.
La main qui a bougé sur le flanc désert.

Nous sommes immobiles depuis longtemps.
Nous parlons bas.
Et le temps reste autour de nous comme des flaques de couleur.

THE BEE, COLOR

Five o'clock.
Light sleep, blurred on the windowpanes.
Day dips into color to bring up the cool,
Streaming water of evening.

And it seems that the soul grows simpler,
Being more of the light, which reassures,
But the One is torn against the obscure leg,
You lose yourself where the mouth has drunk of acrid death.

(The horn of plenty with its red fruit
In the turning sun. And the bee-like humming
Of a sweet, impure eternity over
The meadow, so near and still so burning.)

EVENING

Streaks of blue and black.
Furrows swerving toward the foot of the sky.
The bed, wide and broken like a flooded river.
—Look, it's already evening,
And the fire speaks near us in the eternity of sage.

EVENING LIGHT

Evening,
These birds vaguely quarreling,
Biting each other—light.
The hand that has moved across the deserted breast.

We've been motionless a long while,
Talking softly.
Time stays around us like pools of color.

39

LA PATIENCE, LE CIEL

Que te faut-il, voix qui reprends, proche du sol comme la sève
De l'olivier que glaça l'autre hiver?
Le temps divin qu'il faut pour emplir ce vase,
Oui, rien qu'aimer ce temps désert et plein de jour.

La patience pour faire vivre un feu sous un ciel rapide,
L'attente indivisée pour un vin noir,
L'heure aux arches ouvertes quand le vent
A des ombres qui rouent sur tes mains pensives.

UNE VOIX

Combien simples, oh fûmes-nous, parmi ces branches,
Inexistants, allant du même pas,
Une ombre aimant une ombre, et l'espace des branches
Ne criant pas du poids d'ombres, ne bougeant pas.

Je t'avais converti aux sommeils sans alarmes,
Aux pas sans lendemains, aux jours sans devenir,
A l'effraie aux buissons quand la nuit claire tombe,
Tournant vers nous ses yeux de terre sans retour.

A mon silence; à mes angoisses sans tristesse
Où tu cherchais le goût du temps qui va mûrir.
A de grands chemins clos, où venait boire l'astre
Immobile d'aimer, de prendre et de mourir.

UNE PIERRE

Un feu va devant nous.
J'aperçois par instants ta nuque, ton visage,
Puis, rien que le flambeau,
Rien que le feu massif, le mascaret des morts.

PATIENCE, THE SKY

What do you need, reviving voice, as close to the soil
As the sap of the olive tree that froze last winter?
Divine time, enough to fill this vase,
Yes, only to love time, deserted, drenched with light.

Patience to bring a fire to life under a fleeting sky,
Undistracted waiting for a dark wine,
An hour of open archways when the wind
Casts shadows that wheel over your pensive hands.

A VOICE

How simple we were, among these branches,
Inexistent, walking with the same step, a shadow
In love with a shadow, and the space of the branches
Not creaking or swaying from the shadowy weight.

I'd converted you to sleep without sudden fears,
To steps without tomorrow, to days without becoming,
To the screech-owl in the thicket when clear night falls,
Turning toward us the eyes of the ongoing earth.

To my silence; to my unsad distress
In which you sought the taste of time ripening.
To great walled pathways where the motionless star
Of loving, of taking, of dying, came to drink.

A STONE

A fire goes before us.
At moments I glimpse your neck, your face,
Then nothing but the torch,
Nothing but the massed fire, the flood-tide of death.

Cendre qui te détaches de la flamme
Dans la lumière du soir,
O présence,
Sous ta voûte furtive accueille-nous
Pour une fête obscure.

LA LUMIÈRE, CHANGÉE

Nous ne nous voyons plus dans la même lumière,
Nous n'avons plus les mêmes yeux, les mêmes mains.
L'arbre est plus proche et la voix des sources plus vive,
Nos pas sont plus profonds, parmi les morts.

Dieu qui n'es pas, pose ta main sur notre épaule,
Ébauche notre corps du poids de ton retour,
Achève de mêler à nos âmes ces astres,
Ces bois, ces cris d'oiseaux, ces ombres et ces jours.

Renonce-toi en nous comme un fruit se déchire,
Efface-nous en toi. Découvre-nous
Le sens mystérieux de ce qui n'est que simple
Et fût tombé sans feu dans des mots sans amour.

UNE PIERRE

Le jour au fond du jour sauvera-t-il
Le peu de mots que nous fûmes ensemble?
Pour moi, j'ai tant aimé ces jours confiants, je veille
Sur quelques mots éteints dans l'âtre de nos cœurs.

Ash fallen from the flame
In the evening light,
O presence,
Take us for darkness and joy
Under your furtive roof.

THE LIGHT, CHANGED

We no longer see each other in the same light,
We no longer have the same eyes or the same hands.
The tree is closer, the voice of the springs more lively,
Our steps are deeper now, among the dead.

God who are not, put your hand on our shoulder,
Sketch out our body with the weight of your return,
Complete the mixing of our souls with these stars,
These woods, these bird-calls, these shadows, these days.

Renounce yourself in us as a fruit bursts open,
Blot us out in you. Unveil for us
The mysterious meaning of what is all so simple
And would have burnt darkly in loveless words.

A STONE

Will the day deep within day
Save the few words we were together?
As for me, I've loved these trustful days so much,
I watch over a few words burnt out in the hearth of our hearts.

UNE PIERRE

Nous prenions par ces prés
Où parfois tout un dieu se détachait d'un arbre
(Et c'était notre preuve, vers le soir).

Je vous poussais sans bruit,
Je sentais votre poids contre nos mains pensives,
O vous, mes mots obscurs,
Barrières au travers des chemins du soir.

LE CŒUR, L'EAU NON TROUBLÉE

Es-tu gaie ou triste?
— Ai-je su jamais,
Sauf que rien ne pèse
Au cœur sans retour.

Aucun pas d'oiseau
Sur cette verrière
Du cœur traversé
De jardins et d'ombre.

Un souci de toi
Qui a bu ma vie
Mais dans se feuillage
Aucun souvenir.

Je suis l'heure simple
Et l'eau non troublée.
Ai-je su t'aimer,
Ne sachant mourir?

A STONE

We walked past those meadows
Where a whole god sometimes dropped from a tree
(And it was a token for us, towards evening).

I pushed you silently,
I felt your weight against our pensive hands,
O you, my dark words,
Gates across the roads of evening.

THE HEART, UNCLOUDED WATER

Are you happy or sad?
—Have I ever known,
Save that nothing weighs
On a heart at peace.

No bird's print
On this roof of glass,
A heart transpierced
By gardens and shadows.

A care for you
Which has drunk my life
But no memory
Among these leaves.

I'm the simple hour
And unclouded water.
Have I loved you well,
Not willing to die?

LA PAROLE DU SOIR

Le pays du début d'octobre n'avait fruit
Qui ne se déchirât dans l'herbe, et ses oiseaux
En venaient à des cris d'absence et de rocaille
Sur un haut flanc courbé qui se hâtait vers nous.

Ma parole du soir,
Comme un raisin d'arrière-automne tu as froid,
Mais le vin déjà brûle en ton âme et je trouve
Ma seule chaleur vraie dans tes mots fondateurs.

Le vaisseau d'un achèvement d'octobre, clair,
Peut venir. Nous saurons mêler ces deux lumières,
O mon vaisseau illuminé errant en mer,

Clarté de proche nuit et clarté de parole,
— Brume qui montera de toute chose vive
Et toi, mon rougeoiement de lampe dans la mort.

«ANDIAM, COMPAGNE BELLE...»

Don Giovanni, 1, 3.

Les lampes de la nuit passée, dans le feuillage,
Brûlent-elles encor, et dans quel pays?
C'est le soir, où l'arbre s'aggrave, sur la porte.
L'étoile a précédé le frêle feu mortel.

Andiam, compagne belle, astres, demeures,
Rivière plus brillante avec le soir.
J'entends tomber sur vous, qu'une musique emporte,
L'écume où bat le cœur introuvable des morts.

THE WORDS OF EVENING

The country of early October had no fruit
Not burst open in the grass, and the birds then
Came with cries of absence and of rubble
On a high, curved hull moving quickly towards us.

My words of evening,
You have the chill of late autumn grapes,
But even now the wine burns in your soul, and I find
My one true warmth in what you have begun.

The ship of a clear October's end
May come. Then we shall mingle these two lights,
O my bright ship wandering at sea,

Clarity of coming night and clarity of speech
—The mist that rises from all living things
And you, the glowing of my lamp in death.

"ANDIAM, COMPAGNE BELLE . . ."

Don Giovanni, 1, 3.

The lamps of the past night, in the leaves,
Are they still burning, and in what country?
The tree darkens at the door, it's evening.
The star has gone ahead of the frail mortal fire.

Andiam, campagne belle, stars, dwellings,
River more shining at evening. I can hear
The foam wash over you, swept on by music,
And in it the hidden heartbeat of the dead.

LE LIVRE, POUR VIEILLIR

Étoiles transhumantes; et le berger
Voûté sur le bonheur terrestre; et tant de paix
Comme ce cri d'insecte, irrégulier,
Qu'un dieu pauvre façonne. Le silence
Est monté de ton livre vers ton cœur.
Un vent bouge sans bruit dans les bruits du monde.
Le temps sourit au loin, de cesser d'être.
Simples dans le verger sont les fruits mûrs.

Tu vieilliras
Et, te décolorant dans la couleur des arbres,
Faisant ombre plus lente sur le mur,
Étant, et d'âme enfin, la terre menacée,
Tu reprendras le livre à la page laissée,
Tu diras, C'étaient donc les derniers mots obscurs.

THE BOOK, FOR GROWING OLD

Transhumant stars; and the shepherd bending
Over earthly happiness; and peace
Such as this insect's intermittent cry,
Shaped by a humble god. Silence
Has climbed from your book towards your heart.
A noiseless wind stirs in the world's noise.
Time smiles in the distance, ceasing to be.
Simple is the ripe fruit in the orchard.

You will grow old
And, fading amid the color of the trees,
Casting a slower shadow on the wall,
Being at last, in your soul, the threatened earth,
You will take the book up where you had left it,
You will say, These were the last obscure words.

Le Dialogue d'Angoisse
et de Désir

I

J'imagine souvent, au-dessus de moi,
Un visage sacrificiel, dont les rayons
Sont comme un champ de terre labourée.
Les lèvres et les yeux sont souriants.
Le front est morne, un bruit de mer lassant et sourd.
Je lui dis: Sois ma force, et sa lumière augmente,
Il domine un pays de guerre au petit jour
Et tout un fleuve qui rassure par méandres
Cette terre saisie fertilisée.

Et je m'étonne alors qu'il ait fallu
Ce temps, et cette peine. Car les fruits
Régnaient déjà dans l'arbre. El le soleil
Illuminait déjà le pays du soir.
Je regarde les hauts plateaux où je puis vivre,
Cette main qui retient une autre main rocheuse,
Cette respiration d'absence qui soulève
Les masses d'un labour d'automne inachevé.

The Dialogue of Anguish and Desire

I

Often I imagine a sacrificial face
Above me, its rays like a field
Of plowed earth. Lips and eyes smiling,
Brow downcast, a low and tedious
Sound of the sea. I say: Be my strength,
And its light burns brighter, it looks down
On a land of war at dawn and the length
Of a flooded river whose meanders reassure
This taken, fertilized earth.

And then I'm surprised that it needed
Such time, such effort. For the fruit
Was already the glory of the trees. And the sun
Already shone on the evening land.
I look at the high plateaus where I can live,
This hand that holds another stony hand,
This breathing of absence that stirs up
The masses of an unfinished autumn plowing.

II

Et je pense à Coré l'absente; qui a pris
Dans ses mains le cœur noir étincelant des fleurs
Et qui tomba, buvant le noir, l'irrévélée,
Sur le pré de lumière—et d'ombre. Je comprends
Cette faute, la mort. Asphodèles, jasmins
Sont de notre pays. Des rives d'eau
Peu profonde et limpide et verte y font frémir
L'ombre du cœur du monde . . . Mais oui, prends.
La faute de la fleur coupée nous est remise,
Toute l'âme se voûte autour d'un dire simple,
La grisaille se perd dans le fruit mûr.

Le fer des mots de guerre se dissipe
Dans l'heureuse matière sans retour.

III

Oui, c'est cela.
Un éboulissement dans les mots anciens.
L'étagement
De tout notre vie au loin comme une mer
Heureuse, élucidée par une arme d'eau vive.

Nous n'avons plus besoin
D'images déchirantes pour aimer.
Cet arbre nous suffit là-bas, qui, par lumière,
Se délie de soi-même et ne sait plus
Que le nom presque dit d'un dieu presque incarné.

Et tout ce haut pays que l'Un très proche brûle,

Et ce crépi d'un mur que le temps simple touche
De ses mains sans tristesse, et qui ont mesuré.

II

And I think of Kore the absent; who took
In her hands the dark, glittering heart of the flowers
And fell, drinking blackness, unrevealed,
On the meadow of light—and shade. I understand
This sin, death. Asphodels and jasmine
Grow in our country. There the banks
Of a clear, green, shallow water make the shadow
Of the world's heart shiver . . . Yes, take the flower.
The sin of cutting it is forgiven us,
The whole soul bends over a simple saying,
The gray wash is lost in the ripened fruit.

The iron of warring words subsides
In the happy stream of matter.

III

Yes, that's it.
A flash in the old words.
All the steps
Of our life rising in the distance like a blessed
Sea, lit by a blade of live water.

We no longer need
Harrowing images in order to love.
That tree over there is enough for us, loosed
From itself by light, knowing nothing
But the almost uttered name of an almost incarnate god.

And this high land burnt by the One in its nearness,

And this white-washed wall that simple time
Touches with its hands that know no sadness
And have made their measure.

IV

Et toi,
Et c'est là mon orgueil,
O moins à contre-jour, ô mieux aimée,
Qui ne m'es plus étrangère. Nous avons grandi, je le sais,
Dans les mêmes jardins obscurs. Nous avons bu
La même eau difficile sous les arbres.
Le même ange sévère t'a menacée.

Et nos pas sont les mêmes, se déprenant
Des ronces de l'enfance oubliable et des mêmes
Imprécations impures.

V

Imagine qu'un soir
La lumière s'attarde sur la terre,
Ouvrant ses mains d'orage et donatrices, dont
La paume est notre lieu et d'angoisse et d'espoir.
Imagine que la lumière soit victime
Pour le salut d'un lieu mortel et sous un dieu
Certes distant et noir. L'après-midi
A été pourpre et d'un trait simple. Imaginer
S'est déchiré dans le miroir, tournant vers nous
Sa face souriante d'argent clair.
Et nous avons vieilli un peu. Et le bonheur
A mûri ses fruits clairs en d'absentes ramures.
Est-ce là un pays plus proche, mon eau pure?
Ces chemins que tu vas dans d'ingrates paroles
Vont-ils sur une rive à jamais ta demeure
« Au loin » prendre musique, « au soir » se dénouer?

VI

O de ton aille de terre et d'ombre éveille-nous.
Ange vaste comme la terre, et porte-nous
Ici, au même endroit de la terre mortelle,
Pour un commencement. Les fruits anciens

IV

And you,
And this is my pride,
O less in half-light, O more beloved,
No longer strange to me. I know, we grew up
In the same dark gardens. We have drunk
The same uneasy water under the trees.
The same stern angel has threatened you.

And our steps are the same, untangling themselves
From the thorns of forgettable childhood, from the same
Impure imprecations.

V

Imagine that the light
Lingered on the earth one evening,
Opening the storm and bounty of its hand,
Whose palm is our place of anguish and hope.
Imagine light a victim
For the saving of a mortal place, under a dark,
Yes, and distant god. The afternoon
Was crimson, a single stroke. Imaginings
Tore themselves in the mirror, turning towards us
The bright silver of their smiling faces.
And we've grown a little older. And happiness
Has ripened its bright fruit in absent branches.
Is that a nearer country, my pure water?
Do these paths you take among thankless words
Lead along a shore now forever your home,
To music "over there," to peace "at night"?

VI

O with your wing of earth and darkness wake us,
Angel wide as the earth, and bring us
Here, to the same spot on the mortal earth,
For a beginning. Let the ancient fruit

Soient notre faim et notre soif enfin calmées.
Le feu soit notre feu. Et l'attente se change
En ce proche destin, cette heure, ce séjour.

Le fer, blé absolu,
Ayant germé dans la jachère de nos gestes,
De nos malédictions, de nos mains pures,
Étant tombé en grains qui ont accueilli l'or
D'un temps, comme le cercle des astres proches,
Et bienveillant et nul,

Ici, où nous allons,
Où nous avons appris l'universel langage,

Ouvre-toi, parle-nous, déchire-toi,
Couronne incendiée, battement clair,
Ambre du cœur solaire.

SUR UNE PIETÀ DE TINTORET

Jamais douleur
Ne fut plus élégante dans ces grilles
Noires, que dévora le soleil. Et jamais
Élégance ne fut cause plus spirituelle,
Un feu double, debout sur les grilles du soir.

Ici,
Un grand espoir fut peintre. Oh, qui est plus réel
Du chagrin désirant ou de l'image peinte?
Le désir déchira le voile de l'image,
L'image donna vie à l'exsangue désir.

Appease our hunger and thirst at last.
Let the fire be our fire. And our waiting change
Into this destiny, this hour, this place.

Iron, absolute wheat,
Having sprouted in the fallow ground of our gestures,
Of our hands, cursed but pure,
And fallen in seeds that have gathered the gold
Of an hour, like the circle of these nearer stars,
Benevolent and void,

Here, where we are going,
Where we have learned the universal tongue,

Open, speak to us, burst,
Burnt crown, bright pulse,
Amber of a solar heart.

ON A PIETÀ BY TINTORETTO

Suffering was never
More elegant in these black iron
Gates, devoured by sun. And never
Was elegance more a spiritual need,
A double fire, standing in the gates of night.

Here,
A great hope was painter. Oh, which is more real,
Yearning sorrow or its painted image?
Yearning tore the veil of the image,
The image gave bloodless yearning life.

UNE VOIX

Toi que l'on dit qui bois de cette eau presque absente,
Souviens-toi qu'elle nous échappe et parle-nous.
La décevante est-elle, enfin saisie,
D'un autre goût que l'eau mortelle et seras-tu
L'illuminé d'une obscure parole
Bue à cette fontaine et toujours vive,
Ou l'eau n'est-elle qu'ombre, où ton visage
Ne fait que réfléchir sa finitude?
—Je ne sais pas, je ne suis plus, le temps s'achève
Comme la crue d'un rêve aux dieux irrévélés,
Et ta voix, comme une eau elle-même, s'efface
De ce langage clair et qui m'a consumé.
Oui, je puis vivre ici. L'ange, qui est la terre,
Va dans chaque buisson et paraître et brûler.
Je suis cet autel vide, et ce gouffre, et ces arches
Et toi-même peut-être, et le doute: mais l'aube
Et le rayonnement de pierres descellées.

ART DE LA POÉSIE

Dragué fut le regard hors de cette nuit.
Immobilisées et séchées les mains.
On a réconcilié la fièvre. On a dit au cœur
D'être le cœur. Il y avait un démon dans ces veines
Qui s'est enfui en criant.
Il y avait dans la bouche une voix morne sanglante
Qui a été lavée et rappelée.

A VOICE

You who are said to drink of this almost absent water,
Remember how it eludes us, and speak to us,
Does the deceiving one, caught at last,
Taste unlike mortal water, and are you
Enlightened by obscure words
Drunk from this spring, and ever-living?
Or is the water only darkness, where your face
Reflects only its own finiteness?
—I don't know, I no longer am, time is fulfilled
Like the flood of a dream of unrevealed gods,
And your voice, itself like water, draws back
From this clear language that has consumed me.
Yes, I can live here. The angel, who is earth,
Inhabits every bush, appearing, burning.
I am this empty altar, this pit, these arches,
And you yourself perhaps, and doubt: but dawn,
Too, and the radiance of unsealed stones.

THE ART OF POETRY

The eyes were dragged up out of this night.
The hands immobilized and dried.
The fever reconciled. The heart has been told
To be the heart. The demon that lived in these veins
Has fled howling.
The dismal, blood-stained voice in this mouth
Has been washed and recalled.

THE LURE
OF THE
THRESHOLD

Dans le leurre
du seuil

1975

*They looked as they had heard
of a world ransomed, or one destroyed."*

THE WINTER'S TALE

Le fleuve

Mais non, toujours
D'un déploiement de l'aile de l'impossible
Tu t'éveilles, avec un cri,
Du lieu, qui n'est qu'un rêve. Ta voix, soudain,
Est rauque comme un torrent. Tout le sens, rassemblé,
Y tombe, avec un bruit
De sommeil jeté sur la pierre.

Et tu te lèves une éternelle fois
Dans cet été qui t'obsède.
A nouveau ce bruit d'un ailleurs, proche, lointain;
Tu vas à ce volet qui vibre . . . Dehors, nul vent,
Les choses de la nuit sont immobiles
Comme une avancée d'eau dans la lumière.
Regarde,
L'arbre, le parapet de la terrasse,
L'aire, qui semble peinte sur le vide,
Les masses du safre clair dans le ravin,
A peine frémissent-ils, reflet peut-être
D'autres arbres et d'autres pierres sur un fleuve.
Regarde! De tout tes yeux regarde! Rien d'ici,
Que ce soit cette combe, cette lueur
Au faîte dans l'orage, ou le pain, le vin,
N'a plus cet à jamais de silencieuse
Respiration nocturne qui mariait

The River

But no, once again
Unfolding the wing of the impossible
You awaken, with a cry,
From the place which is only a dream. Your voice
Abrupt, harsh as a flood. All the gathered
Meaning falls into it, with a sound
Of sleep thrown over stone.

And you get up one eternal time
In this summer that haunts you.
Once more the sound of an elsewhere, near, far;
You go to the vibrating blinds . . . Outside,
No wind, the things of night are still
As a thrust of water in the light.
Look,
The tree, the low terrace wall,
The field that seems painted on nothing,
The masses of light sandstone in the ravine,
Are barely trembling, perhaps the reflection
Of other trees and stones in a river.
Look! Look your eyes out! Nothing here,
Not this glen, not this flash
Of the storm at its crest, nor the bread nor the wine,
Has kept that forever of silent
Nocturnal breathing that wedded

Dans l'antique sommeil
Les bêtes et les choses anuitées
A l'infini sous le manteau d'étoiles.
Regarde,
La main qui prend le sein,
En reconnaît la forme, en fait saillir
La douce aridité, la main s'élève,
Médite son écart, son ignorance,
Et brûle retirée dans le cri désert.
Le ciel brille pourtant des mêmes signes,
Pourquoi le sens
A-t-il coagulé au flanc de l'Ourse,
Blessure inguérissable qui divise
Dans le fleuve de tout à travers tout
De son caillot, comme un chiffre de mort,
L'afflux étincelant des vies obscures?
Tu regardes couler le fleuve terrestre,
En amont, en aval la même nuit
Malgré tous ces reflets qui réunissent
Vainement les étoiles aux fruits mortels.

Et tu sais mieux, déjà, que tu rêvais
Qu'une barque chargée de terre noire
S'écartait d'une rive. Le nautonier
Pesait de tout son corps contre la perche
Qui avait pris appui, tu ignorais
Où, dans les boues sans nom du fond du fleuve.

O terre, terre,
Pourquoi la perfection du fruit, lorsque le sens
Comme une barque à peine pressentie
Se dérobe de la couleur et de la forme,
Et d'où ce souvenir qui serre le cœur
De la barque d'un autre été au ras des herbes?
D'où, oui, tant d'évidence à travers tant
D'énigme, et tant de certitude encore, et même
Tant de joie, préservée? Et pourquoi l'image
Qui n'est pas l'apparence, qui n'est pas
Même le rêve trouble, insiste-t-elle
En dépit du déni de l'être? Jours profonds,

Countless benighted beasts and things
In ancient sleep
Under the cloak of the stars.
Look,
The hand that touches the breast,
That recognizes its form, that reveals
Its soft aridity, lifted away,
Considers its own remoteness, its ignorance,
Withdrawn, it burns in the empty cry.
Yet the sky is lit by the same signs,
Why has meaning
Coagulated on the flank of the Bear,
An incurable wound, a clot
Like the cipher of death, that divides
The glittering rush of dark lives
In the river of all through all?
You watch the earthly river flow
Upstream, downstream in the same night
Despite all these reflections that join
The stars, in vain, with mortal fruit.

And you recall more clearly, now, that you dreamed
Of a boat loaded with black earth
Setting out from some shore. The pilot
Leaned his full weight on the pole
Which had touched bottom, you did not know
Where, in the nameless mud of the river-bed.

O earth, earth,
Why the perfection of fruit, if meaning,
Like a boat almost unguessed-at,
Eludes color and form; and this memory
That grips the heart, of a boat
From another summer, level with the grass,
Where does it come from? And how,
Yes, how is such evidence through so much
Enigma, and so much certainty, even so much
Joy preserved? And why is the image
That is not appearance, that is not even
The mist of dreams, so insistent
Against the denial of being? Deep days,

Un dieu jeune passait à gué le fleuve,
Le berger s'éloignait dans la poussière,
Des enfants jouaient haut dans le feuillage,
Rires, batailles dans la paix, les bruits du soir,
Et l'esprit avait là son souffle, égal . . .

Aujourd'hui le passeur
N'a d'autre rive que bruyante, noire
Et Boris de Schloezer, quand il est mort
Entendant sur l'appontement une musique
Dont ses proches ne savaient rien (était-elle, déjà,
La flûte de la délivrance révélée
Ou un ultime bien de la terre perdue,
« Œuvre », transfigurée?)—derrière soi
N'a laissé que ces eaux brûlées d'énigme.
O terre,
Étoiles plus violentes n'ont jamais
Scellé l'orée du ciel de feux plus fixes,
Appel plus dévorant de berger dans l'arbre
N'a jamais ravagé été plus obscur.

. . . .

Terre,
Qu'avait-il aperçu, que comprenait-il,
Qu'accepta-t-il?
Il écouta, longtemps,
Puis il se redressa, le feu
De cette œuvre qui atteignait,
Qui sait, à une cime
De déliements, de retrouvailles, de joie
Illumina son visage.

Bruit, clos,
De la perche qui heurte le flot boueux,
Nuit
De la chaîne qui glisse au fond du fleuve.
Ailleurs,
Là où j'ignorais tout, où j'écrivais,
Un chien peut-être empoisonné griffait
L'amère terre nocturne.

A young god forded the river,
The shepherd went off into the dust,
Children played high in the leaves, laughter,
Quarrels in the stillness, the sounds of evening,
And there the mind breathed, easily . . .

Today the ferryman
Finds no shore that is not black, raging
And Boris de Schloezer, when he died
Hearing music from the landing
That his near ones could not hear (was it
The flute of revealed deliverance already,
Or a last gift from the lost earth,
A "work," transfigured?)—left behind only
These waters burnt by the enigma.
O earth,
Never have more violent stars sealed the verge
Of the sky with such fixed fires, never
Has a more consuming call from the shepherd in the tree
Ravaged so dark a summer.

. . . .

Earth,
What had he seen, understood,
Accepted?
He listened, long,
Then drew himself up, the fire
Of that work which reached,
Who knows, a summit
Of release, recovery, joy
Shone in his face.

Closed sound
Of the pole striking the muddy stream,
Darkness
Of the chain slipping to the bottom.
Elsewhere,
In the place of my ignorance, my writing,
A dog that may have been poisoned
Clawed at night's bitter earth.

Dans le leurre de seuil

Heurte,
Heurte à jamais.

Dans le leurre du seuil.

A la porte, scellée,
A la phrase, vide.
Dans le fer, n'éveillant
Que ces mots, le fer.

Dans le langage, noir.

Dans celui qui est là
Immobile, à veiller
A sa table, chargée
De signes, de lueurs. Et qui est appelé

Trois fois, mais ne se lève.

. . . .

Dans le rassemblement, où a manqué
Le célébrable.

The Lure of the Threshold

Knock,
Knock forever.

In the lure of the threshold.

At the sealed door,
At the empty phrase.
In iron, awakening
Only the word, iron.

In speech, blackness.

In he who sits
By night, motionless
At his table, laden
With signs, glimmers. And is called

Three times, but does not get up.

. . . .

In the gathering, that failed
Of celebration.

Dans le blé déformé
Et le vin qui sèche.

Dans la main qui retient
Une main absente.

Dans l'inutilité
De se souvenir.

Dans l'écriture, en hâte
Engrangée de nuit

Et dans les mots éteints
Avant même l'aube.

. . . .

Dans la bouche qui veut
D'une autre bouche
Le miel que nul été
Ne peut mûrir.

Dans la note qui, brusque,
S'intensifie
Jusqu'à être, glaciaire,
Presque la passe

Puis l'insistance de
La note tue
Qui désunit sa houle
Nue, sous l'étoile.

Dans un reflet d'étoile
Sur du fer.
Dans l'angoisse des corps
Qui ne se trouvent.

Heurte, tard.

In the deformed wheat,
The parching wine.

In the hand that holds on
To an absent hand.

In the uselessness
Of recollection.

In writing, hastily
Garnered at night

And in words that die out
Before dawn.

. . . .

In the mouth that asks
Another mouth
For honey no summer
Can ripen.

In the abrupt note
That grows louder until,
Glacial, it almost
Becomes the crossing

Then the insistence
Of the hushed note
That releases its naked
Swell, under the star.

In the star's gleam
On iron.
In the anguish of bodies
Not finding each other.

Knock, late.

Les lèvres désirant
Même quand le sang coule,

La main heurtant majeure
Encore quand
Le bras n'est plus que cendre
Dispersée.

. . . .
. . . .

Plus avant que le chien
Dans la terre noire
Se jette en criant le passeur
Vers l'autre rive.
La bouche pleine de boue,
Les yeux mangés,
Pousse ta barque pour nous
Dans la matière.
Quel fond trouve ta perche, tu ne sais,
Quelle dérive,
Ni ce qu'éclaireront, saisis de noir,
Les mots du livre.

Plus avant que le chien
Qu'on recouvre mal
On t'enveloppe, passeur,
Du manteau des signes.
On te parle, on te donne
Une ou deux clefs, la vaine
Carte d'une autre terre.
Tu écoutes, les yeux déjà détournés
Vers l'eau obscure.
Tu écoutes, qui tombent,
Les quelques pelletées.

Plus avant que le chien
Qui est mort hier
On veut planter, passeur,
Ta phosphorescence.

Lips wanting
Even as the blood flows,

The fist knocking
Most imperatively when
The arm is no more than
Scattered ashes.

. . . . ; . .
. . . .

Further than the dog
In the black earth
The ferryman rushes, crying
Toward the far shore.
Mouth filled with mud,
Devoured eyes,
Drive your boat for us
Into matter.
What bottom, what drift your pole may find,
You do not know,
Nor what, seized with blackness, the words
Of the book will light up.

Further than the dog
Under its thin cover,
They wrap you, ferryman,
In a cloak of signs.
They advise you, they give you
A key, two keys, the vain
Map of another earth.
You listen, your eyes already turned
To the dark water.
You listen, and the last few
Shovelfuls fall.

Further than the dog
That died yesterday,
Ferryman, they would plant
Your phosphorescence.

Les mains des jeunes filles
Ont dégagé la terre
Sous la tige qui porte
L'or des grainées futures.
Tu pourrais distinguer encore leurs bras
Aux ombres lourdes,
Le gonflement des seins
Sous la tunique.
Rire s'enflamme là-haut
Mais tu t'éloignes.

Tu fus jeté sanglant
Dans la lumière,
Tu as ouvert les yeux, criant,
Pour nommer le jour,
Mais le jour n'est pas dit
Que déjà retombe
La draperie du sang, à grand bruit sourd,
Sur la lumière.
Rire s'enflamme là-haut,
Rougeoie dans l'épaisseur
Qui se désagrège.
Détourne-toi des feux
De notre rive.

Plus avant que le feu
Qui a mal pris
Est placé le témoin du feu, l'indéchiffré,
Sur un lit des feuilles.
Faces tournées vers nous,
Lecteurs de signes,
Quel vent de l'autre face, inentendu,
Les fera bruire?
Quelles mains hésitantes
Et comme découvrant
Prendront, feuilletteront
L'ombre des pages?
Quelles mains méditantes
Ayant comme trouvé?

The hands of young girls
Have loosened the earth
From the stem that bears
The gold of future seed.
You can still see the heavy
Shadows of their arms,
The swelling of breasts
Under the tunic.
Laughter flares above you
But you move away.

You were thrown bleeding
Into the light.
You opened your eyes, crying,
To name the day.
But the day was hardly uttered
When the curtain of blood
Fell again, with a huge dull sound
Over the light.
Laughter flares above you
Glowing in the thickness
That is breaking up.
Turn away
From the fires of our shore.

Further than the fire
That barely burns,
The witness of fire, the undeciphered,
Is laid on a bed of leaves.
Faces turned toward us,
Readers of signs,
What wind from the other face, unheard,
Will make them rustle?
What hesitant hands,
As if finding, grasping,
Leafing through the darkness
Of the pages? What hands
Meditating, as if
They had found what?

. . . .

Oh, penche-toi, rassure,
Nuée
Du sourire qui bouge
En visage clair.

Sois pour qui a eu froid
Contre la rive
La fille de Pharaon
Et ses servantes,

Celles dont l'eau, encore
Avant le jour,
Reflète renversée
L'étoffe rouge.

. . . .

Et comme une main trie
Sur une table
Le grain presque germé
De l'ivraie obscure

Et sur l'eau du bois noir
Prenant se double
D'un reflet, où le sens
Soudain se forme,

Accueille, pour dormir
Dans ta parole,
Nos mots que le vent troue
De ses rafales.

. . . .

Oh, bend down, comfort,
Cloud
Of a smile stirring
In a bright face.

Be for him who shivered
Against the shore
Pharaoh's daughter
And her serving-girls

Whom the water, even
Before daybreak,
Reflects reversed
In their red dresses.

. . . .

And as a hand sorts
On a table
The nearly sprouted wheat
From the dark tares

And pausing on the water
Of black wood, is doubled,
A reflection where meaning
Suddenly forms,

Receive, to sleep
In your speech,
Our words riddled
By the wind's blast.

. . . .

« Es-tu venu pour boire de ce vin,
Je ne te permets pas de le boire.
Es-tu venu pour apprendre ce pain
Sombre, brûlé du feu d'une promesse,
Je ne te permets pas d'y porter lumière.
Es-tu venu ne serait-ce que pour
Que l'eau t'apaise, un peu d'eau tiède, bue
Au milieu de la nuit après d'autres lèvres
Entre le lit défait et la terre simple,
Je ne te permets pas de toucher au verre.
Es-tu venu pour que brille l'enfant
Au-dessus de la flamme qui le scelle
Dans l'immortalité de l'heure d'avril
Où il peut rire, et toi, où l'oiseau se pose
Dans l'heure qui l'accueille et n'a pas de nom,
Je ne te permets pas d'élever tes mains au-dessus de l'âtre où je règne
    clair.

Es-tu venu,
Je ne te permets pas de paraître.
Demandes-tu,
Je ne te permets pas de savoir le nom formé par tes lèvres. »

. . . .

Plus avant que les pierres
Que l'ouvrier
Debout sur le mur arrache
Tard, dans la nuit.

Plus avant que le flanc du corbeau, qui marque
De sa rouille la brume
Et passe dans le rêve en poussant un cri
Comble de terre noire.

"Though you come to drink of this wine,
I will not let you drink it.
Though you come wanting to understand
This dark bread, burnt by the fire of a promise,
I will not let you bring light to it.
Though you come only to quench your thirst
With water, a little warm water, drunk
After other lips in the middle of the night
Between the unmade bed and the simple earth,
I will not let you touch the glass.
Though you come so that the child can shine
Above the flame that seals him
In the deathlessness of the April hour
When he may laugh, and you may, and the bird alights
In the nameless hour that welcomes it,
I will not let you lift your hands above the hearth of my bright
    kingship.

Though you come,
I will not let you appear.
Though you ask,
I will not let you know what name your lips form."

. . . .

Further than the stones
That the workman, standing
On the wall, tears away
Late, in the night.

Further than the crow's flank, that marks
The mist with its rusty stain
And passes into the dream letting out a cry
Full of black earth.

Plus avant que l'été
Que la pelle casse,
Plus avant que le cri
Dans un autre rêve,

Se jette en criant celui qui
Nous représente,
Ombre que fait l'espoir
Sur l'origine,

Et la seule unité, ce mouvement
Du corps—quand, tout d'un coup,
De sa masse jetée contre la perche
Il nous oublie.

. . . .

Nous, la voix que refoule
Le vent des mots.
Nous, l'œuvre que déchire
Leur tourbillon.
Car si je veins vers toi, qui as parlé,
Gravats, ruissellements,
Échos, la salle est vide.
Est-ce « un autre », l'appel qui me répond,
Ou moi encore?
Et sous la voûte de l'écho, multiplié
Suis-je rien d'autre
Qu'une de ses flèches, lancée
Contre les choses?

Nous
Parmi les bruits,
Nous
L'un d'eux.

Se détachant
De la paroi qui s'éboule,
Se creusant, s'évasant,

Further than summer
Broken by the spade,
Further than the cry
Into another dream,

The one who stands for us
Rushes, crying,
A shadow that hope has thrown
Against origin,

And the only oneness, this movement
Of the body when—now leaning
His full weight on the pole,
He forgets us.

. . . .

We, the voice driven back
By the wind of words.
We, the work torn apart
By their whirling.
For if I come to you, who have spoken,
Rubble, streamings,
Echoes, the room is empty.
Is it "another," this call that answers me,
Or, again, myself?
And, multiplied under the echo's arch,
Am I no more
Than one of its arrows
Shot into things?

We
Among the noises,
We
One of them.

Detached
From the crumbling wall,
Hollowed, splayed out,

Se vidant de soi,
S'empourprant,
Se gonflant d'une plénitude lointaine.

. . . .

Regarde ce torrent,
Il se jette en criant dans l'été désert
Et pourtant, immobile,
C'est l'attelage cabré
Et la face aveugle.
Écoute.
L'écho n'est pas autour du bruit mais dans le bruit
Comme son gouffre.
Les falaises du bruit,
Les entonnoirs où se brisent ses eaux,
La saxifrage
S'arrachent de tes yeux avec un cri
D'aigle, final.
Où heurte le poitrail de la voix de l'eau,
Tu ne peux l'entendre,
Mais laisse-toi porter, œil ébloui,
Par l'aile rauque.

Nous
Au fusant du bruit,
Nous
Portés.

Nous, oui, quand le torrent
A mains brisées
Jette, roule, reprend
L'absolu des pierres.

Le prédateur
Au faîte de son vol,
Criant,
Se recourbe sur soi et se déchire.
De son sein divisé par le bec obscur

Emptied,
Reddening,
Swelling with a distant fullness.

. . . .

Look at this flooded stream,
It rushes howling into empty summer
And yet, motionless,
It is a harnessed team rearing
And a blind face.
Listen.
The echo is not around the noise but in the noise,
Its hollow depth.
The cliffs of noise,
The narrows where its waters break,
The saxifrage
Tear from your sight with a final
Eagle's cry.
Where the breast of the voice of water strikes,
You cannot hear it,
But be upborne, dazzled eye,
By the raucous wing.

We
In the burst of noise,
We
Upborne.

We, when the flood
With broken hands
Hurls, rolls, retrieves
The absolute of stones.

The predator
At the peak of its flight,
Crying out,
Bends back and tears itself.
From the breast cleft by the dark beak

Jaillit le vide.
Au faîte de la parole encore le bruit,
Dans l'œuvre
La houle d'un bruit second.
Mais au faîte du bruit la lumière change.

. . . .

Tout le visible infirme
Se désécrit,
Braise où passe l'appel
D'autres campagnes

Et la foudre est en paix
Au-dessus des arbres,
Sein où bougent en rêve
Sommeil et mort,

Et brûle, une couleur,
La nuit du monde
Comme s'éploie dans l'eau
Noire, une étoffe peinte

Quand l'image divise
Soudain le flux,
Criant son grain, le feu,
Contre une perche.

. . . .

Heure
Retranchée de la somme, maintenant.
Présence
Détrompée de la mort. Ampoule
Qui s'agenouille en silence
Et brûle
Déviée, secouée
Par la nuit qui n'a pas de cime.

The void spills out.
At the peak of speech there is still noise,
In the work
The swell of a second noise.
But at the peak of noise the light changes.

. . . .

All the wavering visible
Unwrites itself,
Embers through which the call
Of other fields passes

And the lightning is at peace
Above the trees,
Breast where sleep and death
Stir in their dreams,

And the night of the world,
A color, burns
Like a painted cloth spreading
In black water

Now, when the image
Divides the flow,
Throwing its seed, fire,
Against a pole.

. . . .

Hour
Cut off from the sum, now.
Presence
Undeceived by death. Bulb
That kneels in silence
And burns
Deflected, shaken
By the summitless night.

Je t'écoute
Vibrer dans le rien de l'œuvre
Qui peine de par le monde.
Je perçois le piétinement
D'appels
Dont le pacage est l'ampoule qui brûle
Je prends la terre à poignées
Dans cet évasement aux parois lisses
Où il n'est pas de fond
Avant le jour.
Je t'écoute, je prends
Dans ton panier de corde
Toute la terre. Dehors,
C'est encore le temps de la douleur
Avant l'image.
Dans la main de dehors, fermée,
A commencé à germer
Le blé des choses du monde.

. . . .
. . . .

Le nautonier
Qui touche de sa perche, méditante,
A ton épaule
Et toi, déjà celui que la nuit recouvre
Quand ta perche recherche mais vainement
Le fond du fleuve,

Lequel est, lequel se perdra,
Qui peut espérer, qui promettre?
Penché, vois poindre sur l'eau
Tout un visage

Comme prend un feu, au reflet
De ton épaule.

I hear you
Vibrate in the nullity of the work
That labors through the world.
I hear the trampling
Of calls
Whose pasture is the burning bulb.
I take up fistfuls of earth
In this smooth-walled splaying out
Where there is no bottom
Before daybreak.
I hear you, I catch
The whole world
In your rope basket. Outside
It is still the time of suffering
Before the image.
In the closed hand of the outside
The wheat of things of the world
Has begun to sprout.

. . . .
. . . .

The pilot
Who touches your shoulder
With his meditative pole,
And you, already the one whom night covers
When your pole seeks, in vain,
The river's bottom,

He who is, he who will perish,
Who can hope, who promise?
Bending down, you see a face
Well up in the water

As a fire kindles, in the reflection
Of your shoulder.

Deux couleurs

Plus avant que l'étoile
Dans le reflet
Creusent deux mains qui n'ont, pour retenir,
Que leur confiance.
Cherchent deux mains, brisées,
Pour mieux que l'or
Et que naisse la vie
De rien qu'un rêve.

O gerbes du reflet
Malgré la boue,
Seuil dans le froissement
De l'eau fermée,
Branches et fruits qui passent
L'eau maçonnée!
Oui, tu es ce pays,
Toi que j'éveille
Comme dans l'eau qu'on trouble, même de nuit,
Le ciel est autre.

Bouge dans l'eau remuée
L'arbre d'étoiles.
Prend, dans le souffle accru,
L'autre lumière.

Two Colors

Further than the star
In the reflection
Two hands delve, having nothing to hold with
But their own trust.
Two hands, broken, search
For better than gold
And that life be born
Of nothing but a dream.

O sheaves of reflection
Despite the mud,
Threshold in the rippling
Of the closed water,
Branches and fruits passing
By the walled water!
Yes, you are this country,
You whom I awaken,
As in troubled water, even at night,
The sky is other.

In the stirred water
The tree of stars quickens,
The other light takes
In the heightened breath.

Et donc, puissance nue,
Je te recueille
Dans mes mains rapprochées
Pour une coupe.
S'écoulent au travers
De mes doigts les mondes,
Mais ce qui monte en nous, mon eau, brûlée,
Veut une vie.

Je te touche des lèvres,
Mon amie,
Je tremble d'aborder, enfant, sommeil,
A cette Égypte.
Feuillages, nuits d'été,
Bêtes, routes du ciel,
Souffles, silencieux, signes, inachevés,
Sont là qui dorment.
—Bois, me dis-tu pourtant,
Au sens qui rêve.

Bois, je suis l'eau, brûlée,
A l'épaule du flux,
Là où gonfle le sein,
Par un reflet d'étoile.
Bois, en reflet.
Aime sur moi, que tu ne peux saisir,
D'une bouche sans fin,
La présence immobile de l'étoile.

J'ai confiance, je bois,
L'eau glisse de mes doigts,
Non, elle brille.
Terres, entr'aperçues,
Herbes d'avant le temps, pierres mûries,
Couleurs autres, jamais
Rêvées si simples,
Je touche à vos épis, lourds, que courbe le flux
Dans la ténèbre.

Et notre cri, soudain,
Défait l'étreinte,

And so I gather you,
Naked strength,
Into the cup
Of my joined hands.
Through my fingers
Worlds run,
But what rises in us, my burnt water,
Wants a life.

I touch you with my lips,
My dear one,
I tremble, child, sleep, to reach
This Egypt.
Leaves, summer nights,
Beasts, paths of the sky,
Silent breaths, signs unfinished,
Are there, asleep.
But you tell me, Drink
Of these dreaming words.

Drink, I am the water,
Burnt by a star's reflection,
At the flood's shoulder,
Where the breast swells.
Drink, in reflection.
Love, upon me, what you cannot take
With an endless mouth,
The star's still presence.

I trust, I drink,
The water slips through my fingers,
No, it shines.
Lands, half-glimpsed,
Grass of beforetimes, ripened stones,
Other colors, simple
Beyond imagining,
I touch your heavy grain, which the flood
Bends in the darkness,

And our sudden cry
Breaks our embrace,

Mais quand tu te répands,
Aube, ce blé demeure.

. . . .

Plus avant que l'étoile
Qui a blanchi
Trouve l'agneau le berger
Parmi les pierres.
Aube sur l'écume, laiteuse,
Des bêtes serrées,
Paix au bout du flot, désuni,
Des piétinements.
Il a fait froid, de la nuit
Reste mêlée à la terre.

Plus avant que l'étoile
Dans ce qui est
Se baigne simple l'enfant
Qui porte le monde.
Il fait nuit encore, mais lui
Est de deux couleurs,
Un bleu qui prend au vert
Du faîte des arbres
Comme un feu se fait clair
Parmi des fruits

Et le rouge des lourdes
Étoffes peintes
Que lavait l'Égyptienne, l'irréveillée,
De nuit, dans l'eau du fleuve,

Quand la perche a heurté,
Est-ce le jour,
Dans la boue de l'image aux yeux déserts
A la parole.

But when your light streams,
Dawn, the wheat stays.

. . . .

Further than the star
That has grown pale
The shepherd finds the lamb
Among the stones.
Dawn over the milky foam
Of the huddled beasts,
Peace at the end of the breaking wave
Of stamping hoofs.
It was cold, some night
Stays mixed with the earth.

Further than the star
In what is,
The child who bears the world
Bathes simply.
It is night still, but he
Is of two colors,
A blue, beginning to mix
With the green of the treetops,
As a fire grows lighter
Among fruits

And a red like the heavy
Painted cloths
The Egyptian girl, the unawakened,
Had washed at night in the river,

When the pole struck,
Was that the day,
Through the mud of the image, those empty eyes,
To a living word.

Deux barques

L'orage qui s'attarde, le lit défait,
La fenêtre qui bat dans la chaleur
Et le sang dans sa fièvre: je reprends
La main proche à son rêve, la cheville
A son anneau de barque retenue
Contre un appontement, dans une écume,
Puis le regard, puis la bouche à l'absence
Et tout le brusque éveil dans l'été nocturne
Pour y porter l'orage et le finir.
—Où que tu sois quand je te prends obscure,
S'étant accru en nous ce bruit de mer,
Accepte d'être l'indifférence, que j'étreigne
A l'exemple de Dieu l'aveugle la matière
La plus déserte encore dans la nuit.
Accueille-moi intensément mais distraitement,
Fais que je n'aie pas de visage, pas de nom
Pour qu'étant le voleur je te donne plus
Et l'étranger l'exil, en toi, en moi
Se fasse l'origine . . . —Oh, je veux bien,
Toutefois, t'oubliant, je suis avec toi,
Desserres-tu mes doigts,
Formes-tu de mes paumes une coupe,
Je bois, près de ta soif,
Puis laisse l'eau couler sur tous nos membres.
Eau qui fait que nous sommes, n'étant pas,

Two Boats

The storm lingering, the unmade bed,
The window knocking in the heat,
Blood beating in its fever: I take back
This hand close to mine in its dream, this ankle
Secured to its ring
On the pier, in sleep's foam,
Take back from absence this glance, this mouth,
And the whole sudden waking in nocturnal summer
To bring the storm to it and make it end.
—Wherever you may be, so dark, when I take you,
The sea's sound having grown louder in us,
Consent to be indifference, that I may embrace
The most desert matter waiting by night,
As God the Blind would do. Receive me
Intensely but abstractedly,
Let me have no face or name for you,
So that being the thief I may give you more
And the stranger, exile, in you, in me,
May become the origin . . . —Oh, I would gladly,
And yet, forgetting you, I am with you,
Only unclench my fingers,
Form my hands into a cup,
I drink, close to your thirst,
Then I let water pour over all our limbs.
Water that gives us being, who are not,

Eau qui prend au travers des corps arides
Pour une joie éparse dans l'énigme,
Pressentiment pourtant! Te souviens-tu,
Nous allions par ces champs barrés de pierre,
Et soudain la citerne, et ces deux présences
Dans leur lumière heureuse un peu voilée?
Regarde comme ils se penchent, eux comme nous,
Est-ce nous qu'ils écoutent, dont ils parlent,
Souriant sous les feuilles du premier arbre
Dans leur lumière heureuse un peu voilée?
Et ne dirait-on pas qu'une lueur
Autre, bouge dans cet accord de leurs visages
Et, riante, les mêle? Vois, l'eau se trouble
Mais les formes en sont plus pures, consumées.
Quel est le vrai de ces deux mondes, peu importe.
Invente-moi, redouble-moi peut-être
Sur ces confins de fable déchirée.

J'écoute, je consens,
Puis j'écarte le bras qui s'est replié,
Me dérobant la face lumineuse.
Je la touche à la bouche avec mes lèvres,
En désordre, brisée, toute une mer.
Comme Dieu le soleil levant je suis voûté
Sur cette eau où fleurit notre ressemblance,
Je murmure: C'est donc ce que tu veux,
Puissance errante insatisfaite par les mondes,
Te ramasser, une vie, dans le vase
De terre nue de notre identité?
Et c'est vrai qu'un instant tout est silence,
On dirait que le temps va faire halte
Comme s'il hésitait sur le chemin,
Regardant par-dessus l'épaule terrestre
Ce que nous ne pouvons ou ne voulons voir.
Le tonnerre ne roule plus dans le ciel calme,
L'ondée ne passe plus sur notre toit,
Le volet, qui heurtait à notre rêve,
Se tait courbé sur son âme de fer.
J'écoute, je ne sais quel bruit, puis je me lève
Et je cherche, dans l'ombre encore, où je retrouve
Le verre d'hier soir, à demi plein.

Water that soaks through parched bodies
For a joy scattered among enigmas,
And yet we knew it! Do you remember,
We were walking over those stone-hedged fields,
And suddenly a cistern, and those two presences
In what other country of empty summer?
See how they bend down, just as we do,
Are they listening to us, talking about us,
Smiling under the leaves of the first tree
In their happy, slightly veiled light?
And doesn't it seem that another brightness
Wakes in the harmony of their faces
And mirthfully joins them? See, the water clouds
But the forms in it are purer, consumed.
Which of these two worlds is the true one
Does not matter. Invent me, increase me
At these limits of the torn fable.

I listen, I consent,
Then I push aside the folded arm
That hides the luminous face from me.
I touch the mouth with my lips—
All disorder, broken, a sea.
Like God the Rising Sun I bend down
Over the water where our likeness flowers,
I murmur: So this is what you want,
Wandering power that the worlds cannot satisfy,
To gather yourself, one life, in the bare
Earthen vessel of our identity?
And, true, for a moment all is silence,
You would think time was about to stop
As if pausing on its way,
Looking over the earthly shoulder
At what we cannot or will not see.
Thunder no longer rolls through the calm sky,
Rain no longer sweeps over our roof,
The blinds that knocked in our dream
Are quiet, turned in on their iron soul.
I hear I don't know what noise, get up
And search, still in the dark, and find
Last night's glass, half full, breathing

Je le prends, qui respire à notre souffle,
Je te fais le toucher de ta soif obscure,
Et quand je bois l'eau tiède où furent tes lèvres,
C'est comme si le temps cessait sur les miennes
Et que mes yeux s'ouvraient, à enfin le jour.

. . . .

Donne-moi ta main sans retour, eau incertaine
Que j'ai désempierrée jour après jour
Des rêves qui s'attardent dans la lumière
Et du mauvais désir de l'infini.
Que le bien de la source ne cesse pas
A l'instant où la source est retrouvée,
Que les lointains ne se séparent pas
Une nouvelle fois du proche, sous la faux
De l'eau non plus tarie mais sans saveur.
Donne-moi ta main et précède-moi dans l'été mortel
Avec ce bruit de lumière changée,
Dissipe-toi me dissipant dans la lumiére.

Les images, les mondes, les impatiences,
Les désirs qui ne savent pas bien qu'ils dénouent,
La beauté mystérieuse au sein obscur,
Aux mains frangées pourtant d'une lumière,
Les rires, les rencontres sur des chemins,

Et les appels, les dons, les consentements,
Les demandes sans fin, naître, insensé,
Les alliances éternelles et les hâtives,
Les promesses miraculeuses non tenues
Mais, tard, l'inespéré, soudain : que tout cela
La rose de l'eau qui passe le recueille
En se creusant ici, puis l'illumine
Au moyeu immobile de la roue.

With us. I pick it up, I let you touch it
With your obscure thirst, and when I drink
The warm water where your lips were
It is as if time had ceased on mine
And my eyes were opened, to the day at last.

. . . .

Give me your unreturning hand, fitful water
That I have disballasted day after day
Of dreams that linger in the light
And the bad longing for infinity.
May the gift of the source not cease
The moment the source is recovered,
May the distances not be cut off once more
From the near, by a scythe of water
Not dried up, then, but savorless.
Give me your hand, go ahead of me
Into mortal summer, with your sound of light changed,
Be scattered as you scatter me in the light.

Images, worlds, longings,
Ignorant desires that yet unbind,
Mysterious beauty with its dark breast
But with hands fringed with light,
Laughter, meetings on the roads,

And the appeals, the gifts, the assents,
The endless demands, this madness, birth,
The eternal and the hurried unions,
The miraculous promises that are not kept
But suddenly, late, the unexpected: that all
Should gather into the rose of flowing water
As it hollows out here, and be made light
And the still hub of the wheel.

. . . .

Paix, sur l'eau éclairée. On dirait qu'une barque
Passe, chargée de fruits; et qu'une vague
De suffisance, ou d'immobilité,
Soulève notre lieu et cette vie
Comme une barque à peine autre, liée encore.
Aie confiance, et laisse-toi prendre, épaule nue,
Par l'onde qui s'élargit de l'été sans fin,
Dors, c'est le plein été; et une nuit
Par excès de lumière; et va se déchirer
Notre éternelle nuit; va se pencher
Souriante sur nous l'Égyptienne.

Paix, sur le flot qui va. Le temps scintille.
On dirait que la barque s'est arrêtée.
On n'entend plus que se jeter, se désunir,
Contre le flanc désert l'eau infinie.

. . . .

Peace, on the bright water. You would think a boat
Was passing by, laden with fruit; that a wave
Of fullness, or of stillness,
Uplifted our place and this life
Almost like the same boat, still moored.
Trust, let yourself go, bare shoulder,
On the swelling wave of endless summer,
Sleep, it is high summer; and one night
By an excess of light; and our eternal darkness
Will soon be broken; the Egyptian girl
Will bend down, smiling, over us.

Peace, on the flowing water. Time sparkles.
You would think the boat had landed.
All you hear now is the infinite water
Heaving and breaking against its bare side.

Le feu, ses joies de sève déchirée.
La pluie, ou rien qu'un vent peut-être sur les tuiles.
Tu cherches ton manteau de l'autre année.
Tu prends les clefs, tu sors, une étoile brille.

Éloigne-toi
Dans les vignes, vers la montagne de Vachères.
A l'aube
Le ciel sera plus rapide.

Un cercle
Où tonne l'indifférence.
De la lumière
A la place de Dieu.

Presque du feu, vois-tu,
Dans le baquet de l'eau de la pluie nocturne.

. . . .

Dans le rêve, pourtant,
Dans l'autre feu obscur qui avait repris,
Une servante allait avec une lampe
Loin devant nous. La lumière était rouge

Fire, the joys of split sap.
Rain, or maybe just wind on the roof-tiles.
You look for your coat from last year.
You take the keys, you go out, a star shines.

Move off
Through the vineyards, towards the mountain
Of Vachères. At dawn
The sky will be quicker.

A circle
Where indifference thunders.
Light
In place of God.

Almost fire, you see,
In the trough of the nocturnal rain.

. . . .

Yet in the dream,
In the other dark fire that flared up again,
A serving-girl went far ahead of us
With a lamp. Its light was red

Et ruisselait
Dans les plis de la robe contre la jambe
Jusqu'à la neige.

Étoiles, répandues.
Le ciel, un lit défait, une naissance.

Et l'amandier, grossi
Après deux ans: le flot
Dans un bras plus obscur, du même fleuve.

. . . .

O amandier en fleurs,
Ma nuit sans fin,
Aie confiance, appuie-toi enfant
A cette foudre.

Branch d'ici, brûlée d'absence, bois
De tes fleurs d'un instant au ciel qui change.

. . . .

Je suis sorti
Dans un autre univers. C'était
Avant le jour.
J'ai jeté du sel sur la neige.

And streamed
Down the folds of the dress against her thigh
Onto the snow.

Star-strewn sky,
An unmade bed, a birth.

And the almond tree, grown
Sturdier in two years: the flow
Of the same river in a darker arm.

. . . .

O flowering almond tree,
My endless night,
Trust, child, lean
Against this lightning.

Branch here, burnt by absence, drink
With your brief flowers from the changing sky.

. . . .

I came out
Into another universe. It was
Before dawn.
I threw salt on the snow.

La terre

Je crie, Regarde,
La lumière
Vivait là, près de nous! Ici, sa provision
D'eau, encore transfigurée. Ici le bois
Dans la remise. Ici, les quelques fruits
A sécher dans les vibrations du ciel de l'aube.

Rien n'a changé,
Ce sont les mêmes lieux et les mêmes choses,
Presque les mêmes mots,
Mais, vois, en toi, en moi
L'indivis, l'invisible se rassemblent.

Et elle! n'est-ce pas
Elle qui sourit là (« Moi la lumière,
Oui, je consens ») dans la certitude du seuil,
Penchée, guidant les pas
D'on dirait un soleil enfant sur une eau obscure.

. . . .

Je crie, Regarde,
L'amandier

The Earth

I cry, Look,
Light
Was living so near us! Its store of water
Is here, still transfigured. Wood
Is here in the shed. Here is some fruit set
To dry in the vibrations of the dawn sky.

Nothing has changed,
These are the same places and the same things,
Almost the same words, but see,
In you, in me, the undivided
And the invisible come together.

And she! is it not
She who smiles there ("I the light,
Yes, I consent") in the certainty of the threshold,
Bending down, guiding the steps
Of what looks like a child-sun over the dark water.

. . . .

I cry, Look,
The almond tree

Se couvre brusquement de milliers de fleurs.
Ici
Le noueux, l'à jamais terrestre, le déchiré
Entre au port. Moi la nuit
Je consens. Moi l'amandier
J'entre paré dans la chambre nuptiale.

Et, vois, des mains
De plus haut dans le ciel
Prennent
Comme passe une ondée, dans chaque fleur,
La part impérissable de la vie.

Elles divisent l'amande
Avec paix. Elles touchent, elles prélèvent le germe.

Elles l'emportent, grainée déjà
D'autres mondes,
Dans l'à jamais de la fleur éphémère.

. . . .

O flamme
Qui consumant célèbres,
Cendre
Qui dispersant recueilles.

Flamme, oui, qui effaces
De la table sacrificielle de l'été
La fièvre, les sursauts
De la main crispée.
Flamme, pour que la pierre du ciel clair
Soit lavée de notre ombre, et que ce soit
Un dieu enfant qui joue
Dans l'âcreté de la sève.
Je me penche sur toi, je rassemble, à genoux,
Flamme qui vas,
L'impatience, l'ardeur, le deuil, la solitude
Dans ta fumée.
Je me penche sur toi, aube, je prends

Suddenly bursts into thousands of flowers.
Here
The gnarled, the forever earthly, the torn
Comes to harbor. I the night
Consent. I the almond tree
Enter the wedding chamber, adorned.

And see, hands
From the height of the sky,
Like a passing
Shower, take from each blossom
The imperishable part of its life.

In peace they break open
The almond. They touch, they lift out the seed.

They bear it away, already sown
With other worlds,
Into the forever of the ephemeral flower.

. . . .

O flame
Who praise in consuming,
Ash
Who in scattering gather.

Flame, yes, who clear
From the sacrificial table of summer
The fever, the spasms
Of the clenched hand.
Flame, that the stone of the bright sky
Be washed of our shadow, and a child god
Be there, playing
In the pungency of the sap.
I bend over you, fleeting flame,
Kneeling I gather
Impatience, passion, grief, solitude
Into your smoke.
I bend over you, dawn, I take

Dans mes mains ton visage. Qu'il fait beau
Sur notre lit désert! Je sacrifie
Et tu es la résurrection de ce que je brûle.

Flamme
Notre chambre de l'autre année, mystérieuse
Comme la proue d'une barque qui passe.

Flamme le verre
Sur la table de la cuisine abandonnée,
A V.
Dans les gravats.

Flamme, de salle en salle,
Le plâtre,
Toute une indifférence, illuminée.

Flamme l'ampoule
Où manquait Dieu
Au-dessus de la porte de l'étable.
Flamme
La vigne de l'éclair, là-bas,
Dans le piétinement des bêtes qui rêvent.
Flamme la pierre
Où le couteau du rêve a tant œuvré.

Flamme,
Dans la paix de la flamme,
L'agneau du sacrifice gardé sauf.

. . . .

Et, tard, je crie
Des mots que le feu accepte.

Je crie, Regarde,
Ici a déposé un sel inconnu.

Je crie, Regarde,
Ta conscience n'est pas en toi,

Your face in my hands. What fair skies
Over our empty bed! I sacrifice
And you are the resurrection of what I burn.

Flame
Our last-year's room, mysterious
As the prow of a passing ship.

Flame the glass
On the table in the deserted kitchen
At V.
In the rubble.

Flame, from room to room,
The plaster,
All indifference, in the daylight.

Flame the bulb
Where God was not
Above the stable door.
Flame
The vine of lightning, there,
In the stamping of dreaming beasts.
Flame the stone
Where the dream's knife has worked so much.

Flame,
In the peace of the flame,
The sacrificial lamb kept safe.

. . . .

And, late, I cry out
Words that the fire accepts.

I cry, Look,
An unknown salt has settled here.

I cry, Look,
Your consciousness is not in you,

L'amont de ton regard
N'est pas en toi,
Ta souffrance n'est pas en toi, ta joie moins encore.

Je crie, Écoute,
Une musique a cessé.
Partout, dans ce qui est,
Le vent se lève et dénoue.
Aujourd'hui la distance entre les mailles
Existe plus que les mailles,
Nous jetons un filet qui ne retient pas.
Achever, ordonner,
Nous ne le savons plus.
Entre l'œil qui s'accroît et le mot plus vrai
Se déchire la taie de l'achevable.
O ratures, ô rouilles
Où la trace de l'eau, celle du sens
Se résorbant s'illimitent,
Dieu, paroi nue
Où l'érosion, l'entaille
Ont même aspect désert au flanc du monde.
Comme il est tard!
On voit un dieu pousser quelque chose comme
Une barque vers un rivage mais tout change.
Effondrements sur la route des hommes,
Piétinements, clameurs au bas du ciel.
Ici l'ailleurs étreint
La main œuvrante
—Mais quand elle dévie dans le trait obscur,
C'est comme une aube.

Regarde,
Ici, sur la lande du sens,
A quelques mètres du sol,
C'est comme si le feu avait pris feu,
Et ce second brasier, dépossession,
Comme s'il prenait feu encore, dans les hauts
De l'étoffe de ce qui est, que le vent gonfle.
Regarde,
Le quatrième mur s'est descellé,
Entre lui et la pile du côté nord

The upflow of your glance
Is not in you,
Your suffering is not in you, much less your joy.

I cry, Listen,
A certain music has ceased.
Everywhere, in what is,
The wind springs up and unbinds.
Today the space between the meshes
Is more real than the meshes,
We cast a net that holds nothing.
To complete, to arrange,
Are no longer within our power.
Between the sharpening eye and the truer word
The veil of the attainable is torn.
O erasures, o stains
Where the traces of water, of meaning,
Reabsorbed, become limitless.
God, a bare wall
Where erosion and deliberate iron
Leave the same empty marks on the side of the world.
How late it is!
You see a god in something like a boat
Pulling for shore, but it all changes.
Cave-ins on the road of men,
Trampling feet, outcries under the sky.
Here elsewhere clutches
The hand at work
—But where the obscure sign swerves off
It is like a dawn.

Look,
Here on the heath of meaning,
A few feet from the ground,
It is as if fire had caught fire,
As if this second bed of coals, dispossession,
Flared up again, on the heights
Of the wind-filled stuff of what-is.
Look,
The fourth wall is unsealed,
Between it and the pile on the north side

Il y a place pour la ronce
Et les bêtes furtives de chaque nuit.
Le quatrième mur et le premier
Ont dérivé sur la chaîne,
Le sceau de la présence a éclaté
Sous la poussée rocheuse.
J'entre donc par la brèche au cri rapide.
Est-ce deux combattants qui ont lâché prise,
Deux amants qui retombent inapaisés?
Non, la lumière joue avec la lumière
Et le signe est la vie
Dans l'arbre de la transparence de ce qui est.

Je crie, Regarde,
Le signe est devenue le lieu.
Sous le porche de foudre
Fendu
Nous sommes et ne sommes pas.
Entre avec moi, obscure,
Accepte par la brèche au cri de faim.

Et soyons l'un pour l'autre comme la flamme
Quand elle se détache du flambeau,
La phrase de fumée un instant lisible
Avant de s'effacer dans l'air souverain.

. . . .

Oui, toutes choses simples
Rétablies
Ici et là, sur leurs
Piliers de feu.

Vivre sans origine,
Oui, maintenant,
Passer, la main criblée
De lueurs vides.

There is space for brambles
And the furtive beasts of each night.
The fourth wall and the first
Have drifted on the chain,
The stony thrust
Has burst the seal of presence.
And I pass through the quick cry of the breach.
Is it two wrestlers who have let go,
Two lovers who fall back unsatisfied?
No, light plays with light
And the sign is life
In the tree of the transparency of what-is.

I cry, Look,
The sign has become the place.
Under the split portal
Of the lightning
We are and are not.
Come in with me, dark one,
Consent at the breach's hungry cry.

And we shall be for each other like the flame
When it leaves the torch,
A phrase of smoke briefly legible
Before it vanishes in the sovereign air.

. . . .

Yes, all simple things
Reestablished
Here and there, on their
Pillars of fire.

To live without origin,
Yes, now,
To pass, our hands riddled
With empty gleams.

Et tout attachement
Une fumée,
Mais vibrant clair, comme un
Airain qui sonne.

. . . .

Retrouvons-nous
Si haut que la lumière comme déborde
De la coupe de l'heure et du cri mêlés,
Un ruissellement clair, où rien ne reste
Que l'abondance comme telle, désignée.
Retrouvons-nous, prenons
A poignées notre pure présence nue
Sur le lit du matin et le lit du soir,
Partout où le temps creuse son ornière,
Partout où l'eau précieuse s'évapore,
Portons-nous l'un vers l'autre comme enfin
Chacun toutes les bêtes et les choses,
Tous les chemins déserts, toutes les pierres,
Tous les ruissellements, tous les métaux.
Regarde,
Ici fleurit le rien; et ses corolles,
Ses couleurs d'aube et de crépuscule, ses apports
De beauté mystérieuse au lieu terrestre
Et son vert sombre aussi, et le vent dans ses branches,
C'est l'or qui est en nous: or sans matière,
Or de ne pas durer, de ne pas avoir,
Or d'avoir consenti, unique flamme
Au flanc transfiguré de l'alambic.

Et tant vaut la journée qui va finir,
Si précieuse la qualité de cette lumière,
Si simple le cristal un peu jauni
De ces arbres, de ces chemins parmi des sources,
Et si satisfaisantes l'une pour l'autre
Nos voix, qui eurent soif de se trouver
Et ont erré côte à côte, longtemps
Interrompues, obscures,

And all attachment
Smoke,
But vibrating brightly
Like a sounding brass.

. . . .

Let us meet again
So high up that light seems to overflow
The cup where the hour and the cry are mixed,
A bright streaming, where nothing remains
But abundance itself, now proclaimed.
Let us meet again, let us take
Our pure naked presence in our hands
On the bed of morning and the bed of evening,
Wherever time digs its rut,
Wherever the precious water evaporates,
Let us come to each other now
As if each of us were all beasts, all things,
All the empty roads, the stones,
The streams, the metals.
Look,
Here nothingness flowers; its inner petals,
Its dawn and twilight colors, its offerings
Of mysterious beauty to the earthly place,
And its dark green and the wind in its branches—
It is the gold within us: immaterial gold,
Gold of impermanence, of non-possession,
Gold of consent given, only flame
On the alembic's transfigured side.

And such is the worth of the dying day,
So precious the quality of its light,
So simple the slightly yellowed crystal
Of these trees, of these paths among the springs,
And so right our voices one
For the other, that had thirsted for this reunion
And wandered side by side, broken off,
Obscured for so long,

Que tu peux nommer Dieu ce vase vide,
Dieu qui n'est pas, mais qui sauve le don,
Dieu sans regard mais dont les mains renouent,
Dieu nuée, Dieu enfant et à naître encore,
Dieu vaisseau pour l'antique douleur comprise,
Dieu voûte pour l'étoile incertaine du sel
Dans l'évaporation qui est la seule
Intelligence ici qui sache et prouve.

. . . .

Et nos mains se cherchant
Soient la pierre nue
Et la joie partagée
La brassée d'herbes

Car bien que toi, que moi
Criant ne sommes
Qu'un anneau de feu clair
Qu'un vent disperse

Si bien qu'on ne saura
Tôt dans le ciel
Si même eut lieu ce cri
Qui a fait naître,

Toutefois, se trouvant,
Nos mains consentent
D'autres éternités
Au désir encore.

. . . .

Et notre terre soit
L'inachevable
Lumière de la faux
Qui prend l'écume

That you might name this empty vase God,
God who is not, but who saves the gift,
Blind God, but whose hands renew,
God a cloud, God a child, a child unborn,
God a vessel for ancient grief now understood,
God a dark sky for the faint star of salt
In the evaporation which is the one
Intelligence that knows and bears witness here.

. . . .

And our hands, reaching
For each other, be the bare
Stone, and our shared joy
An armful of grass

For though you and I
Crying out are only
A ring of bright fire
Scattered by the wind

So that soon no one
Will know, in the sky,
That there ever was this cry
Which led to birth,

Even so, having found
Each other, our hands consent
To yield to desire's
Eternities again.

. . . .

And our earth be
The unattainable
Light of the scythe
That takes the foam

Et non parce qu'est vraie
Sa seule foudre,
Bien que le vide, clair,
Soit notre couche

Et que toi près de moi,
Simples, n'y sommes
Que fumée rabattue
Du sacrifice,

Mais pour sa retombée
Qui nous unit,
Blé de la transparence,
Au désir encore.

. . . .

Éternité du cri
De l'enfant qui semble
Naître de la douleur
Qui se fait lumière.

L'éternité descend
Dans la terre nue
Et soulève le sens
Comme une bêche.

. . . .

Et vois, l'enfant
Est là, dans l'amandier,
Debout
Comme plusieurs vaisseaux arrivant en rêve.

Il monte
Entre lune et soleil. Il essaie de pencher vers nous
Dans la fumée

And not because only
Its lightning is true,
Although the bright void
Is our bed

And you and I, simple,
Side by side there,
Are only the smoke
Of that stifled sacrifice,

But for its falling back
Which unites us,
Wheat of transparency,
To desire again.

. . . .

Eternity of the cry
Of the child who seems
Born of a suffering
That turns to light.

Eternity descends
Into the bare earth
And brings up meaning
Like a spade.

. . . .

And see, the child
Is there, in the almond tree,
Standing
Like several ships landing in a dream.

He climbs
Between sun and moon. He tries to bend
His mirthful fire,

Son feu, riant,
Où l'ange et le serpent ont même visage.
Il offre
Dans la touffe des mots, qui a fleuri,
Une seconde fois du fruit de l'arbre.

Et déjà le maçon
Se penche vers le fond de la lumière.
Sa bêche en prend les gravats
Pour le comblement impossible.

Il racle
De sa bêche phosphorescente
Cet autre ciel, il fouille
De son fer antérieur à notre rêve
Sous les ronces,
A l'étage du feu et de l'incréé.
Il arrache
La touffe blanche du feu
Au battement de l'incréé parmi les pierres.

Il se tait.
Le midi de ses quelques mots est encore loin
Dans la lumière.

Mais, tard,
Le rouge déteint du ciel
Lui suffira, pour l'éternité du retour
Dans les pierres, grossies
Par l'attraction des cimes encore claires.

. . . .

N'étant que la puissance du rien,
Le bouche, la salive du rien,
Je crie,

Et au-dessus de la vallée de toi, de moi
Demeure le cri de joie dans sa forme pure.

Where angel and serpent have the same face,
Towards us in the smoke.
He offers
In the tuft of words, which has flowered,
The fruit of the tree for a second time.

And the mason already
Stoops towards the depth of the light.
His spade takes up its rubble
For the impossible fulfilling.

He scrapes
This other sky with his phosphorescent
Spade, he digs
With its iron older than our dream
Under the brambles,
To the level of fire and the uncreated.
He tears up
The white tuft of fire
From the pulsing of the uncreated among the stones.

He says nothing.
The midday of his few words is still
Far off in the light.

But, late,
The faded red of the sky
Will suffice him, for the eternity of the return
Among the stones, increased
By the attraction of the still bright hilltops.

. . . .

Being only the power of nothingness,
The mouth, the spittle of nothingness,
I cry out,

And above the valley of you, of me
The cry of joy remains in its pure form.

. . . .

Oui, moi les pierres du soir, illuminées,
Je consens.

Oui, moi la flaque
Plus vaste que le ciel, l'enfant
Qui en remue la boue, l'iris
Aux reflets sans repos, sans souvenirs,
De l'eau, moi, je consens.

Et moi le feu, moi
La pupille du feu, dans la fumée
Des herbes et des siècles, je consens.

Moi la nuée
Je consens. Moi l'étoile du soir
Je consens.
Moi les grappes de mondes qui ont mûri,
Moi le départ
Des maçons attradés vers les villages,
Moi le bruit de la fourgonnette qui se perd,
Je consens. Moi le berger,
Je pousse la fatigue et l'espérance
Sous l'arche de l'étoile vers l'étable.
Moi la nuit d'août,
Je fais le lit des bêtes dans l'étable.
Moi le sommeil,
Je prends le rêve dans mes barques, je consens.

Et moi, la voix
Qui a tant désiré. Moi le maillet
Qui heurta, à coups sourds,
Le ciel, la terre noire. Moi le passeur,
Moi la barque de tout à travers tout,
Moi le soleil,
Je m'arrête au faîte du monde dans les pierres.

. . . .

Yes, I the stones of evening, light-struck,
Consent.

Yes, I the pool
Wider than the sky, the child
Stirring up its mud, the iris
In the restless, unmemoried reflections
Of the water, consent.

And I the fire,
The pupil of the fire's eye, in the smoke
Of grass and centuries, consent.

I the cloud
Consent. I the evening star
Consent.
I the bunches of ripened worlds,
I the departure
Of masons going home late to the villages,
I the fading noise of the truck,
Consent. I the shepherd
Drive weariness and hope to stable
Under the archway of the star.
I the August night
Bed the beasts down in the stable.
I, sleep,
Take the dream aboard my boats, I consent.

And I, the voice
Of so much desire, I the mallet
That struck the sky and the black earth
With dull blows. I the ferryman,
I the boat of all through all,
I the sun,
Stop at the world's height among the stones.

Parole
Décrucifiée. Chanvre de l'apparence
Enfin rouie.

Patience
Qui a voulu, et su.
Couronne
Qui a droit de brûler.

Perche
De chimères, de paix,
Qui trouve
Et touche doucement, dans le flux qui va,

A une épaule.

Speech
Uncrucified. Hemp of appearance
Retted at last.

Patience
That has willed and known.
Crown
With the right to burn.

Pole
Of chimeras, of peace,
That finds
In the quick of the flow and gently touches

A shoulder.

Les nueés

Deux fois silencieuse l'après-midi
Par vertu de l'été désert, et d'une flamme
Qui déborde, on ne sait si de ce vase
Ou de plus haut encore dans le ciel.

Nous avons donc dormi : je ne sais combien
D'étés dans la lumière; et je ne sais
Non plus dans quels espaces nos yeux s'ouvrent.
J'écoute, rien ne vibre, rien ne finit.

A peine le désir façonnant l'image
Tourne-t-il méditant, sur son axe simple,
L'argile d'un éveil en rêve, trempée d'ombre.

Toutefois le soleil bourdonne sur la vitre
Et, l'âme enveloppée de ses rouges élytres,
Il descend, mais en paix, vers la terre des morts.

. . . .

Au-dessus de moi seul, quand je traçais
Le signe d'espérance en temps de guerre,
Une nuée rôdait noire et le vent
Dispersait à grandes lueurs la phrase vaine.

The Clouds

Twice silent the afternoon
By virtue of empty summer, and of a flame
Overflowing, is it from this vase
Or from somewhere higher in the sky?

So we've slept: I don't know how many
Summers in the light; and I don't know
In what spaces our eyes are opening.
I listen, nothing vibrates, nothing ends.

Desire shaping the image, lost in thought,
Barely turns, on its simple axis, the clay
Of a dreamt awakening, soaked with darkness.

Yet the sun buzzes at the windowpane
And, its soul wrapped in its red elytra,
Drops, but peacefully, toward the land of the dead.

. . . .

Above me alone, when I drew the sign
Of hope in a time of war,
A cloud prowled blackly and the wind
In great flashes scattered the useless phrase.

Au-dessus de nous deux, qui avons voulu
Le nœud, le déliement, une énergie
S'accumula entre deux hauts flancs sombres
Et il y eut, enfin,
Comme un tressaillement dans la lumière.

Autres pays, montagnes éclairées
Du ciel, lacs au-delà, inapprochés, nouvelles
Rives,—apaisement des dieux progéniteurs,
L'éclair aura été sa propre cause

Et au-dessus de l'enfant à ses jeux
L'anneau de ces nuages, le feu clair
Qui semble s'attarder ce soir, comme une preuve.

. . . .

Nuages, oui,
L'un à l'autre, navires à l'arrivée
Dans un rapport de musique. Il me semble, parfois,
Que la nécessité se métamorphose
Comme à la fin du *Conte d'hiver*
Quand chacun reconnaît chacun, quand on apprend
De niveau en niveau dans la lumière
Que ceux qu'avaient jetés l'orgueil, le doute
De contrées en contrées dans le dire obscur
Se retrouvent, se savent. Parole en cet instant
Leur silence; et silence leurs quelques mots
On ne sait si de joie ou de douleur
« Bien qu'à coup sûr l'extrême de l'une ou l'autre ».
Ils semblent, dit encore
Un témoin, méditant, et qui s'éloigne,
Entendre la nouvelle
D'un monde rédimé ou d'un monde mort.

Nuages,
Et ces deux pourpres là-bas un père, une fille,
Et cet autre plus proche, la statue
D'une femme, mère de la beauté, mère du sens,

Above the two of us, who have willed
The knot and the loosing, an energy
Gathered between two high, looming flanks
And there was, finally,
Something like a shuddering in the light.

Other countries, mountains lit by the sky,
Lakes beyond them, unapproached, new
Shores,—appeasement of the god-progenitors,
The lightning-flash will have been its own cause

And above the child at play
The ring of these clouds, the bright fire
That seems to linger this evening, like a proof.

. . . .

Clouds, yes,
One with the others, ships arriving
In musical intervals. It seems to me, at times,
That necessity is metamorphosed
As at the end of *The Winter's Tale*
When they all recognize one another, when you see
From level to level in the light
That those who have been cast by pride and doubt
From place to place in their idle talk
Find and know themselves. Their silence in that moment
Speaks; and their few words are silence
Whether from joy or sorrow who can say
"But in the extremity of the one it must needs be."
They looked, the witness also said,
Grown thoughtful, on his way
Away, "as they had heard of a world
Ransomed, or one destroyed."

Clouds,
And two of them crimson, a father, a daughter,
And, closer, a third, the statue of a woman,
Mother of beauty, mother of meaning,

Dont on voit bien qu'immobile longtemps,
Étouffée dans sa voix de siècle en siècle,
Déniée, animée
Par rien que la magie de la sculpture,
Elle prend vie, elle va parler. Foudre ses yeux
Qui s'ouvrent dans le gouffre du safre clair,
Mais foudre souriante comme si,
Condamnée à suivre le rêve au flux stérile
Mais découvrant de l'or dans le sable vierge,
Elle avait médité et consenti.
L'homme d'ailleurs s'approche, son visage
Déchiré s'apaisant de tant de joie.
Il gravit les degrés de l'heure qui roule
En rafales, car le ciel change, la nuit vient,
Et vacille où elle l'attend, nuit étoilée
Qui s'ébrase, musique. Il se redresse,
Il se tourne vers l'univers. Ses traits scintillent
De la phosphorescence de l'absolu,
Et le jour reprend pour eux tous et nous, comme une veine
Se regonfle de sang,—cime des arbres
Crevassée par l'éclair, fleuves, châteaux
En paix de l'autre rive. Oui, une terre
Sur ses colonnes torses de nuée.

Et qu'importe si l'homme, le ciel tournant,
Vacille une seconde fois, dit à la femme
A demi emportée déjà, nuage noir,
Quelques mots que l'on n'entend pas puis se détourne,
S'éloigne à ses côtés qui se dissipent
Et se penche vers elle
Et cache son visage en pleurs dans ses mains pures

Puisque vers l'Occident, encore clair,
Un navire à fond plat, dont la proue figure
Un feu, une fumée, est apparu,
Livre rouvert, nuage rouge, au faîte
De la houle qui s'enfle. Il vient,
Il vire, lentement, on ne voit pas
Ses ponts, ses mâts, on n'entend pas les cris
De l'équipage, on ne devine pas
Les chimères, les espérances de ceux qui

Who you see, though she has been motionless
A long time, her voice stifled
From age to age, denied, animated
Only by the magic of sculpture,
Is coming to life, and will speak. Lightning
Her eyes opening in the abyss of bright sandstone,
But lightning that smiles as if, condemned
To follow the sterile flow of a dream
But finding gold in the virgin sand,
She had taken thought and consented.
Then the man approaches, his harrowed
Face softening at so much joy.
He climbs the steps of the hour that flees
In bursts, for the sky changes, night is coming,
And wavers where she awaits him, starry night
Opening wide, music. He straightens up,
He turns toward the universe. Its features glitter
With the phosphorescence of the absolute,
And day recovers for them and for us,
Like a vein filling with blood again—a summit
Of trees crevassed by lightning, rivers,
Castles peaceful on the far shore. Yes,
An earth upheld on its columns of cloud.

And what matter if the man, under the turning sky,
Wavers a second time, says to the woman
Who is already half swept away, a black cloud,
Some words no one hears and then turns,
Draws back from her as she begins to vanish,
And leans to her
And hides his weeping face in her pure hands

Since from the West, which is still light,
A flat-bottomed ship, its prow a figure
Of fire, of smoke, comes into view,
A reopened book, a red cloud, at the crest
Of the swelling wave. It approaches,
Tacks about slowly, you cannot see
Its decks, its masts, cannot hear the shouts
Of its crew, cannot guess
The chimeras, the hopes of the men

Là-haut se pressent à l'avant, les yeux immenses,
Ni quel autre horizon ils aperçoivent,
Quelle rive peut-être, on ne sait non plus
De quelle ville incendiée ils ont dû fuir,
De quelle Troie inachevable; mais on sent
Battre dans ce bras nu toute l'ardeur
De l'été, notre angoisse ... Aie foi, le sens
Peut croître dans tes mots, terre sauvée,
Comme la transparence dans la grappe
De l'été, celui qui vieillit. Parles-tu, chantes- tu, enfant,
Et je rêve aussitôt que toute la treille
Terrestre s'illumine; et que ce poids
Des étoiles serrées à du froid, des pierres
Denses comme des langues non révélées,
Et des cimes que prend notre nuit encore,
Des cris de désespoir mais des cris de joie,
Des vies qui se séparent dans l'énigme,
Des erreurs, des effondrements, des solitudes
Mais des aubes aussi, des pressentiments,
Des eaux qui se dénouent au loin, des retrouvailles,
Des enfants qui jouent clair à des proues qui passent,
Des feux dans les maisons ouvertes, des appels
Le soir, de porte en porte dans la paix,
Oui, que ce vrai, ce lieu déjà, presque le bien,
Mûrit, que ce n'était que la grappe verte.

Tout n'est-il pas si cohérent, si prêt
Bien que, certes, scellé? Le soleil de l'aube
Et le soleil du soir, l'illuminé,
Mènent bien, bœufs aveugles, la charrue
De l'or universel inachevé,
Et sonne sur leur front cette chaîne d'astres
Indifférents, c'est vrai: mais eux avancent
Comme une eau s'évapore, un sel dépose
Et n'est-ce toi là-bas, mère dont les yeux brillent,
Terre, qui les conduis,
La robe rouge déchirée, non, entrouverte
Sous l'arche de l'étoile première née?

Mais toujours et distinctement je vois aussi
La tache noire dans l'image, j'entends le cri
Qui perce la musique, je sais en moi

Crowded at the bow, wide-eyed,
Nor what new horizon they glimpse,
What shore perhaps, nor do you know
What burning city they are fleeing from,
What unattainable Troy; but you feel
All of summer's heat, our anguish, beating
In that bare arm . . . Have faith, redeemed earth,
A sense may grow in your words, as transparency
Grows in the grapes of aging summer.
When you speak or sing, child,
Immediately I dream that the whole earthly arbor
Is shining; and that this weight
Of stars huddled in the cold, of stones
Dense as unrevealed tongues, of peaks
Still wrapped in our night, of cries of despair
And cries of joy, of lives parted
In the enigma, of mistakes, breakdowns, solitudes,
But of dawns, too, of premonitions,
Of waters unraveling in the distance, of reunions,
Of children playing brightly on passing bows,
Of fires in the open houses, of calls
At evening, from door to door in the stillness,
That this truth, this place, this almost good,
For long a green cluster, is ripening now.

It is all so coherent, isn't it, so ready
Though, of course, still sealed? The morning sun
And the evening sun, the illuminated, two
Blind oxen, indeed pull the plow
Of universal, unattained gold,
And, true, a chain of stars clinks on their foreheads,
Indifferent stars: yet they keep on
As water evaporates, as a salt settles out
And is it not you there, mother with bright eyes,
Earth, who drive them,
Your red dress torn, no, parted slightly,
Under the arch of the firstborn star?

But always and distinctly I also see
The black stain in the image, I hear
The cry that pierces the music, and know

La misère du sens. Non, ce n'est pas
Aux transfigurations que peut prétendre
Notre lieu, en son mal. Je dis l'espoir,
Sa joie, son feu même de grappe immense, quand
L'éclair de chaque nuit frappe à la vitre, quand
Les choses se rassemblent dans l'éclair
Comme au lieu d'origine, et les chemins
Luiraient dans les jardins de l'éclair, la beauté
Y porterait ses pas errants . . . Je dis le rêve,
Mais ce n'est que pour le repos de mots blessés.

Et je sais même dire; et je suis tenté
De vous dire parfois, signes fiévreux,
Criants, les salles peintes,
Les cours intérieures ombragées,
La suffisance de l'été sur les dalles fraîches,
Le murmure de l'eau comme absente, le sein
Qui est semblable à l'eau, une, infinie,
Gonflée d'argile rouge. De vous donner
L'anneau des ciels de palmes, mais aussi
Celui, lourd, de cette cheville, qu'une main
De tiédeur et d'indifférence fait glisser
Contre l'arc du pied maigre, cependant
Que la bouche entrouverte ne cherche que
La mémoire d'une autre. « Regarde-moi,
Dirait la voix néante à travers la mienne,
Je mens, à l'infini, mais je satisfais,
Je ne suis pas mais je ferme les yeux,
Je courbe si tu veux ma nuque noire
Et je chante, veux-tu, esprit lassé,
Ou je feins de dormir » . . . Au crépuscule
La guêpe se couronne de lumière,
Elle règne absolue dans son instant
D'ascension tâtonnante sur la grappe.
Non, nous ne sommes pas guéris du jardin,
De même que ne cesse pas, gonflé d'une eau
Noire, l'épanchement du rêve quand les yeux s'ouvrent.
Encore nous chargerons, à contre-jour
Dans l'afflux d'en dessous, étincelant,
Notre barque à fond plat de fruits, de fleurs
Comme d'un feu, rouge, dont la fumée

In myself the poverty of meaning. No,
Our place, in its darkness, can make no claim
To transfigurations. I speak of hope,
Its joy, even its fire, like a full cluster
Of grapes, when the lightning each night strikes
The window, when things would gather in the flash
As in the place of origin, and the paths would shine
In the gardens of lightning, and beauty turn
Her wandering step there . . . I speak of the dream,
But only so that wounded words may rest.

And I can even speak, and am sometimes tempted
To speak to you, feverish signs,
Crying out, of great painted halls,
Shaded inner courtyards, summer's fullness
On the cool flagstones, the murmur
As of absent water, the breast
That is like water, one, infinite,
Swollen with red clay. To give you
A ring of palm-tree skies, but also
This heavy ring at the ankle, that a warm
And indifferent hand slips over the arch
Of a lean foot, even though
The half-opened mouth seeks only
The memory of another. "Look at me,"
The voice that is nothing would say through mine,
"I lie, infinitely, yet I please you,
I am not, yet I shut my eyes,
If you wish I will bend my dark neck,
I will sing, if you wish, weary spirit,
Or feign sleep . . ." At dusk
The wasp is crowned with light, she reigns
Absolute over the cluster of grapes
In her moment of groping ascension.
No, we're not cured of the garden, any more
Than the dream's outpouring, swollen with black
Water, ceases when we open our eyes.
In the half-light of the glittering
Rush from below, we shall still load
Our flat-bottomed boat with fruit, with flowers
Like a red fire, whose smoke

Dissipera de ses âcres images
Les heures et les rives. Et que d'espoirs
Enfantins, sous les branches! Quelle avancée
Dans les mots consentants! Bien que la nuit
Nous frôle même là d'une aile insue
Et trempe même là son bec, dans l'eau rapide.

. . . .

« Je voulais l'enrichir de n'être qu'une image
Pour que lui n'en soit qu'une, et que le feu
Du temps, s'il prend aux corps, aux cris, aux rêves même,
Laisse intacte la forme où nous nous retrouvions,

Aussi je me faisais sa réserve d'eau pure,
J'illimitais ses yeux qui se penchaient sur moi,
Ma bouche aimait sa bouche aux hâtives confiances,
C'était ma joie d'attendre et de lui faire don.

—Il dort. Je suis l'étoffe de la porte
Que l'on a trempée d'eau pour changer de ciel,
J'ourle l'après-midi d'outre-marine,
Je suis le jeu des quelques ombres sur son corps.

Il vieillit. Même en nous l'heure a grossi et roule
Son bruit de nuit qui vient dans les pierres. Parfois
Il laisse aller son bras dans cette eau plus froide,
Je ne sais si en rêve et ne me sachant pas . . . »

. . . .

« Es-tu venu pour ce livre fermé,
Je ne consens pas que tu l'ouvres.
Es-tu venu pour en briser le sceau
Brûlant, troué de nuit, courbé, feuillage
Sous l'orage qui rôde et n'éclate pas,
Je ne te permets pas d'en toucher la cire.

Will scatter its acrid images along
The hours and shores. And what childish hopes
Under the branches! What a journey on
Among consenting words! Though night, even there,
Brushes us with an unnoticed wing
And dips its beak, even there, in the quick water.

. . . .

"My wish was to be but an image, and to make him
An image, too, so that time's fire,
Though it take bodies, cries, even dreams, would leave
Untouched the form in which we knew ourselves,

So I made myself his store of pure water,
I unbounded his eyes that were bent on me,
My mouth loved his mouth's furtive trustings,
My joy was to wait and give myself to him.

—He sleeps. I am the curtain in the doorway
That was soaked with water to change the sky,
I hem the afternoon in ultramarine,
I am the play of a few shadows on his body.

He grows older. Even in us the hour has filled out
And rolls its noise of coming night among the stones.
At times he lets his arm trail in this colder water,
Perhaps in dream, perhaps forgetting me . . ."

. . . .

"Though you come for this closed book,
I will not allow you to open it.
Though you come to break the seal,
Burning, pitted with night, bent, leaves
Under the prowling threat of a storm,
I will not let you touch the wax.

Es-tu venu « ne serait-ce que pour »
Entrevoir, comme en songe, une parole
Croître transfigurée dans l'aube du sens
(Et je sais bien qu'un soc a travaillé
Longtemps à cet espoir et, retombé
Dans la phrase terrestre, brille là
Déchiré au rebord de ma lumière),
Je reste silencieux dans ta voix qui rêve . . .
Es-tu venu pour dévaster l'écrit
(Tout écrit, tout espoir), pour retrouver
La surface introublée que double l'étoile
Et boire à l'eau qui passe et te baigner
Sous la voûte où mûrit le fruit non le sens
Je ne t'ai pas permis d'oublier le livre. »

. . . .

O rêves, beaux enfants
Dans la lumière
Des robes déchirées,
Des épaules peintes.

« Puisque rien n'a de sens,
Souffle la voix,
Autant peindre nos corps
De nuées rouges.

Vois, j'éclaire ce sein
D'un peu d'argile
Et délivre la joie, qui est le rien,
D'être la faute. »

. . . .

Ils marchent, les pieds nus
Dans leur absence,
Et atteignent les rives
Du fleuve terre.

Though you come 'only in order to' glimpse,
As in a dream, how speech can be
Metamorphosed in the dawn of meaning
(And I know that a ploughshare has worked
A long time in that hope and, fallen back
Into the earthly phrase, shines there
Devastated at the edge of my light), listen,
I am silent in your dreaming voice . . .
Though you come to lay waste the writing
(All writing, all hope), in order to recover
The unclouded surface that reflects the star,
To drink of the passing water and to bathe
Under the vault where fruit, not meaning, ripens,
I have not allowed you to forget the book."

. . . .

O dreams, fine children
In the light
Of torn dresses,
Of painted shoulders.

"Since life has no meaning,"
Breathes the voice,
"It's enough if we paint
Our bodies with red clouds.

See, I brighten this breast
With a little clay
And set joy, which is nothingness,
Free of sin."

. . . .

They walk, barefooted
In their absence,
And come to the banks
Of the river earth.

Ils demandent, ils donnent,
Les yeux fermés,
Les chevilles rougies
Par la boue d'images.

Rien n'aura précédé, rien ne finit,
Ils partagent, une eau,
S'étendent, le flanc nu
Reflète l'étoile.

Ils passent, prenant part
A l'eau étincelante,
A toi, pierre jetée,
A des mondes là-bas, qui s'élargissent.

. . . .

Et à leurs pas se joint
Flore la pure
Qui jette ses pavots
A qui demande.

Et beauté pastorale
Nue, pour ouvrir
A des bêtes mouillées, au froid du jour,
L'enclos du simple

—Mais aussi beauté grise
Des fumées
Qui se tord et défait
Au moindre souffle

Et la folle qui parle
Par plusieurs bouches
Et, penchée, qui secoue
Sa chevelure . . .

They ask, they give,
Their eyes closed,
Their heels reddened
With the clay of images.

Nothing will have come before,
Nothing ends, they share
The water, they lie down,
The bare flank reflects the star.

They pass, taking part
In the sparkling water,
In you, skipped stone,
In worlds widening away.

. . . .

And they're joined on the way
By Flora, the pure one,
Who throws her poppies
To whoever asks.

And pastoral beauty,
Naked, to open
To the damp beasts, in morning's chill,
The fold of the simple.

—But also the gray
Beauty of smoke
That writhes and unravels
At the slightest breath

And the mad girl who speaks
With many mouths,
And, bending down, shakes
Her disheveled hair . . .

. . . .

« Tu ne me toucheras
Ni d'été ni d'hiver,
Ni quand la lune croît
Ou se dissipe.

Ni des mains du désir
Ni en image,
Ni de bouche qui aime
Ou déchirée.

Dormiras-tu,
Je reviendrai pourtant
Contre tes lèvres,

Te retourneras-tu
En soupirant
Comme pour te pencher, mon voyageur,
Sur une source,

Je serai là,
Ta bouche frôlera mes paupières closes. »

. . . .
. . . .

Ici, la tâche
Que je ne sais finir. Ici, les mots
Que je ne dirai pas.

Ici, la flaque
Noire, dans la nuée.
Ici, dans le regard,
Le point aveugle.

. . . .

"You shall not touch me
Summer or winter,
Not when the moon waxes
Nor when it wanes.

Neither with longing hands
Nor in image,
Neither with a loving mouth
Nor with a torn.

But should you sleep
I will come to meet
Your lips again,

Should you turn over
Sighing
As if to bend down, my voyager,
To a spring,

I will be there,
Your lips will brush my closed eyelids."

. . . .
. . . .

Here is the task
I cannot finish. Here, the words
I will not speak.

Here, the black
Pool, in the storm-cloud.
Here, the blind spot
In the glance of the eye.

. . . .

Mais, vois,
Nos fenêtres là-bas sont éclairées
Par tout de même encore un soleil du soir
Et nos vitres sont comme une eau, troublées
Mais aussi transmutées, coagulées
Par le bras méditant de la lumière.
L'énigme, le soleil rêvé, la barque rouge
Passe, boitant sa mort. Mais ce pays
Est, calme, son sillage, où la maison
Se révèle l'étoile, qui s'élève
Pour la paix au-dessus des herbes, dans le souffle
Égal enfin, des dieux du jardin désert.
Approchons-nous. De près les vitres s'éteignent,
Mais l'or se retirant à son autre rive
A laissé à fleurir dans leur sable vierge
Le rien, qui est la vigne. Oh, penche-toi, appuie
Ton front contre la vitre! C'est le bien,
Tout lieu où naître vient dans le flux sans trêve,
Vois croître le vrai fruit, toi qui consens,
Vois ses rinceaux briller dans la salle sombre.

Tu te penches, tu prends
Un peu de la divinité d'une herbe sèche
Et dans la profusion de l'odeur froissée
Cesse l'attente de la vie au cri de faim.
Des lèvres qui demandent d'autres lèvres,
De l'eau qui veut la pente dans les pierres,
De l'élan de l'agneau, fait de joie pure,
De l'enfant qui joue sans limite sur le seuil
Tu accomplis le vœu puisque tu accueilles
La terre, qui excède le désir.

Tu te penches . . . Le myrte, puis pleurer,
Mon amie, ce n'est là que l'été qui vibre
Comme fait un volet que le vent assaille
Sur son gond d'espérance déchirée.
Mais que ce jour est clair! Notre révolte
Est bue par la porosité de la lumière,

. . . .

But, see,
There, all the same, our windows
Are still lit by the evening sun
And our windowpanes are like water, clouded
But also transmuted, coagulated
By the meditative arm of the light.
The enigma, the dreamt sun, the red boat
Passes, limping its death. But this calm
Country is its wake, where the house
Reveals itself as the star, that rises
For peace above the grasses, in the breathing,
Even at last, of the gods of the empty garden.
Go nearer. Up close the windows lose their light,
But the gold, withdrawing to its far shore,
Has left the vine, nothingness, to flower
In the virgin sand. Oh, lean forward, rest
Your forehead on the glass! This is the good,
Each place where birth rises in the ceaseless flow,
See truth's vine growing, you who consent,
See its branches shining in the dim hall.

You bend down, you pick
A little of the divinity of a dry herb
And in the abundance of its crushed odor
This waiting which is life, this cry of hunger, ends.
Of lips that ask for other lips,
Of water that seeks a slope among the stones,
Of the lamb's leaping, which is pure joy,
Of the child playing infinite on the threshold,
You fulfill the vow since you accept
The earth which exceeds desire.

You bend down . . . Myrtle, then weeping,
My dear, that is only summer trembling
As a windowblind when the wind assaults it
Trembles on the torn hope of its hinge.
But how bright the day is! Our revolt
Is soaked up by the porosity of the light,

Et l'assombrissement de l'aile du ciel,
Son cri, le vent qui recommence, tout cela
Dit la vie enfin prête à soi et non la mort.
Vois, il aura suffi de faire confiance,
L'enfant a pris la main du temps vieilli,
La main de l'eau, la main des fruits dans le feuillage,
Il les guide muets dans le mystère,
Et nous qui regardons de loin, tout nous soit simple
De croiser son regard qui ne cille pas.

. . . .

Désir se fit Amour par ses voies nocturnes
Dans le chagrin des siècles; et par beauté
Comprise, par limite acceptée, par mémoire
Amour, le temps, porte l'enfant, qui est le signe.

Et en nous et de nous, qui demeurons
Si obscurs l'un à l'autre, ce qui est
La faute mais fatale, la parole
Étant inachevée comme l'être encor,

Que sa joie prenne forme: pour retenir
L'eau dans sa coupe fugitive; pour refléter
Le feu, qui est le rien; pour faire don
D'au moins l'idée du sens—à la lumière.

. . . .

Nuages,
Et un, le plus au loin, oui, à jamais
Rouge, l'eau et le feu
Dans le vase de terre, la fumée
En tourbillons au point de braise pure
Où va bondir la flamme . . . Mais ici
Le sol, comme le ciel,
Est parsemé à l'infini de pierres

And the sky's wing darkening over, its cry,
The wind picking up again, all of this speaks
Of life at last ready for itself, not of death.
You see, trusting will have been enough,
The child has taken aged time by the hand,
And the water, and the fruit among the leaves,
He leads them silently into the mystery,
And, for us who watch from afar,
May it all be simple
To meet his unblinking glance.

. . . .

Desire became Love on its nocturnal ways
Through the grief of the ages; and through beauty
Understood, through limits accepted, through memory
Love, time, has brought the child, who is the sign.

And in us and of us, who remain
So dark to each other, which is the one sin
But inescapable, our human speech
As yet unfinished, like being itself,

May its joy take form: to hold
The water in its fleeting cup; to reflect
The fire, which is nothingness; to offer
At least the idea of meaning—to the light.

. . . .

Clouds,
And one, the most distant, yes,
Forever red, water and fire
In the earthen vessel, swirls
Of smoke around the glowing center
Where a flame will leap up . . . But here
The ground, like the sky,
Is strewn to infinity with stones

Dont quelques-unes, rouges,
Portent des traits que nous rêvons des signes.

Et nous les dégageons des mousses, des ronces,
Nous les prenons, nous les soulevons. Regarde!
Ici, c'est un tracé, de l'écriture,
Ici vibra le cri sur le gond du sens,
Ici . . . Mais non, cela ne parle pas, l'entaille
Dévie, au faîte
Aussi de braise pure, dans l'esprit,
Où la répétition, la symétrie
Auraient redit l'espoir d'une main œuvrante.

Le silence
Comme un pont éboulé au-dessus de nous
Dans le soir.

Nous ramassons pourtant,
Mon amie,
Tant et plus de ces pierres, quand la nuit
Tachant l'étoffe rouge, trouant nos voix,
Les dérobe déjà à nos mains anxieuses.

Et nuées que nous sommes, leur feu nous guide
Quand nous rentrons, chargés,
A la maison, « là-bas ». Quand nous passons
Déserts
Dans la vitre embrasée de ce pays
Qui ressemble au langage: illuminé
Au loin, pierreux ici. Quand nous allons
Plus loin même, nous divisant, nous déchirant,
L'enfant courant devant nous dans sa joie
A sa vie inconnue,

Simples,—non, clairs,

En paix,
Immobiles parfois à des carrefours,
Entre les colonnes des feux de l'été qui va prendre fin,
Dans l'odeur de l'étoile et de la cendre.

Some of which, red,
Bear marks that we dream are signs.

And we pick them from the moss, the brambles,
We take them and hold them up. Look!
There is a line here, some kind of script,
Here a cry trembled on the hinge of meaning,
Here . . . But no, it says nothing, the mark
Swerves off, this too,
Among the glowing embers, in the mind,
Where repetition, symmetry
Would have kept the memory of a writing hand.

Silence
Like a fallen bridge above us
In the evening.

And yet, my dear,
We gather so many
And still more of these stones, when night
Staining the red cloth, muffling our voices,
Already hides them from our anxious hands.

And clouds that we are, their fire guides us
When we come back, weighted down,
To the house, "yonder." When we pass
Vacant
In the flaming window of this country
That resembles language: brightly lit
In the distance, stony here. When we go
Further still, wearing, breaking down,
The child running ahead of us in his joy
To his unknown life,

Simple,—no, clear,

Peaceful,
Motionless sometimes at the crossroads,
Between the columns of fire of the summer that is ending,
In the odor of star and ash.

. . . .

« Tout cela », oui,
Nos leurres, nos joies,
Nos regrets à jamais,
Non, nos consentements, nos certitudes,

Tout cela, c'est l'été,
L'incohérent
Qui assaille nos yeux
De son eau brusque.

Et dehors c'est la nuit,
Non, c'est le jour
Qui proclame, glaireux,
Une naissance.

. . . .

L'été:
Cette chevèche que cloue
Là, sur le seuil,
Le fer en paix de l'étoile.

. . . .

"All of that," yes,
Our enticements, our joys,
Our endless longings,
No, our consents, our certainties,

All of that is summer,
The incoherent
That assaults our eyes
With its sudden water.

And outside it is night,
No, it is day,
Glairy, proclaiming
A birth.

. . . .

Summer:
This screech-owl
Nailed to the threshold
By the star's peaceful iron.

L'épars, l'indivisible

Oui, à la vitre
Dans un essai de fuir
A heurts sourds
—Criant parfois
Par une tête plus haut.

Oui, dans la nuit
Où la télévision cherche le rivage,
Où l'antique espérance se penche sur
Les lèvres de l'image,
Mord
Dans la solitude du sang
L'épaule nue de l'image.

Oui, par la nuit
Où le besoin de sens presse longtemps
Le sein froid de l'image
Et seul, le cœur serré,
Se détourne, sous les constellations du vain désir.

The Scattered, the Indivisible

Yes, at the window
In an effort to escape
Knocking dully
—Sometimes shouting
Through a higher head.

Yes, in the night
When the television seeks the shore,
When ancient hope bends over
The lips of the image,
Bites
In the solitude of blood
The bare shoulder of the image.

Yes, by the night
When the need for meaning has clutched so long
The cold breast of the image
And alone, heartsick,
Turns away, under the constellations of vain desire.

. . . .

Oui, par le dieu
Qui erre sous l'apparence d'un agneau
Près de la fourgonnette,
Sous l'ampoule qui brûle toute la nuit.
Je m'arrête, il s'arrête,
J'avance, et ce visage

Se dissipe, éclairant

Ma jambe, qui le pousse
Dans le givre qui crisse au-dehors du monde.

. . . .

Oui, par la voix
Violente contre le silence de,
Par le heurt de l'épaule
Violemment contre la distance de
—Mais de ta foudre d'indifférence tu partages,
Ciel soudain noir,
Le pain de notre solitude sur la table.

. . . .

Oui, par la porte qui vibre
Du souffle
De l'apparence trouée
(Et si je sors je serai aveugle
Dans la couleur).

Oui, par la vibration qui parfois
Semble finir.
Oui, par la fièvre qui reprend tard dans le monde.

. . . .

Yes, by the god
Who wanders in the guise of a lamb
Beside the truck,
Under the bulb that burns all night.
I stop, he stops,
I approach, and the face

Vanishes, lighting up

My leg, that pushes it
Away into the night-frost of the world outside.

. . . .

Yes, by the violent
Voice against the silence of,
Through the violent lunge
Of the shoulder against the distance of,
—But with your lightning of indifference,
Sudden black sky, you break
The bread of our solitude at the table.

. . . .

Yes, by the door that vibrates
At the breath
Of shattered appearance
(And if I go out I will be
Blind, in the color).

Yes, by the vibration that sometimes
Seems to end.
Yes, by the fever that rises again late in the world.

. . . .

Oui, par le soir
Quand il remue les cendres de la couleur,
Hâtant à mains d'aveugle
Le montée de la flamme sans lumière.

(La foudre,
L'arbre qui a crié sur sa gorge nue,
Et toi
Ce qui demeure du ciel.)

. . . .

Oui, par la cime éclairée
Une heure encore.

Oui, par la main
Qui trace violemment le trait de la cime
Sans fin,
Sans avenir,
Parfois noyé d'une encre claire, parfois sombre

Et sans place dans la lumière qui va seule.

. . . .

Oui, par ces jours
Où errait le tonnerre, dès avant l'aube.
Par mes chemins dans les herbes mouillées
Qu'avait courbées la nuit sous ses roues de pierre.

Oui, par les ronces
Des cimes dans les pierres. Par cet arbre, debout
Contre le ciel.
Par les flammes, partout,

. . . .

Yes, by the evening
When it stirs the ashes of color,
Hastening with a blind man's hands
The climbing of the lightless flame.

(Lightning,
The tree that cried out on its bare breast,
And you
What is left of the sky.)

. . . .

Yes, by the summit lit
An hour longer.

Yes, by the hand
That violently draws the line of the summit
Without end,
Without future,
Sometimes drenched in bright ink, sometimes dim

And placeless in the light that goes on alone.

. . . .

Yes, by those days
When thunder roamed about, long before dawn.
By my paths in the damp grass
That night had crushed under its wheels of stone.

Yes, by the brambles
Among the stones of the summit. By this tree, standing
Against the sky.
By the flames, everywhere,

Et les voix, chaque soir,
Du mariage du ciel et de la terre

(Tard, quand l'éponge pousse sur la table
Qui brille un peu
Les débris du pain et du vin.)

. . . .

Oui, par les deux colonnes de bois
Abandonnées,
Oui, par le sel
Durci, dans la boîte de la cuisine peinte de noir,
Oui, par le sac de plâtre : ouvert, durci,
Grain de l'impossédable, qui illumine.

Oui, par le trou
Près de la cheminée, béant encore
(Et la pioche et la pelle sont restées là
Contre le mur : le maçon, appelé,
A peine est-il passé, silencieux,
A un autre travail dans une autre salle.)

. . . .

Oui, par ce lieu
Perdu, non dégagé
Des ronces, puis des cendres d'un espoir.
Par ce désir vaincu, non, consumé

Car nous aurons vécu si profond les jours
Que nous a consentis cette lumière !
Il faisait beau toujours, beau à périr,
La campagne alentour était déserte,
Nous n'entendions que respirer la terre
Et grincer la chaîne du puits, cause du temps
Qui retombait du seau comme trop de ciel.

And the voices, each night,
Of the marriage of sky and earth

(Late, when the sponge wipes from the table
Which shines a little
The remains of bread and wine.)

. . . .

Yes, by the two wooden columns
Abandoned,
Yes, by the salt
Caked in its black painted box in the kitchen,
Yes, by the sack of plaster: open, hardened,
Seed of the unpossessible, enlightening.

Yes, by the hole
Still gaping, next to the chimney
(The pick and shovel are leaning there
Against the wall: as if the mason
Had been called away, and had gone silently
To another task in another room.)

. . . .

Yes, by this lost
Place, not cleared
Of brambles, or of the ash of hope.
By this desire overcome, no, consumed

For we have so deeply lived the days
That were granted us by this light!
They were days beautiful beyond belief,
The country around us was deserted,
We heard only the breathing of the earth
And the chain creaking in the well, drawing up
Time that spilled from the bucket

Nous travaillions ici ou là, dans de grandes salles,
Nous ne parlions que peu, à voux rouillée
Comme on cache une clef sous une pierre.
Parfois la nuit venait, du bout des longes,
Parfaite femme voûtée de noir poussant muettes
Ses bêtes dans les eaux du soleil constant.

Et qu'elle dorme
Dans l'absolu que nous avons été
Cette maison qui fut comme un ravin
Où bruit le ciel, où vient l'oiseau qui rêve
Boire la paix nocturne . . . Irrévélée,
Trop grande, trop mystérieuse pour nos pas,
Ne faisons qu'effleurer son épaule obscure,
Ne troublons pas celle qui puise d'un souffle égal
Aux réserves de songe de la terre.
Déposons simplement, la nuit venue, ces pierres
Où nous lisions le signe, à son flanc désert.

Que de tâches inachevables nous tentions,
Que de signes impénétrables nous touchions
De nos doigts ignorants et donc cruels!
Que d'errements et que de solitude!
La mémoire est lassée, certes, le temps étroit,
Le chemin infini encore . . . Mais le ciel
A des pierres plus rougeoyantes du côté
Du soir, et dans nos vies qui font étape,
Lumière qui t'accrois parfois, tu prends et brûles.

. . . .

Oui, par la nuit
Là-haut, dans notre chambre de l'été
Qui va comme une barque, hésitant parfois
Dans l'écume du ciel (et je te vois
Encore, dans la glace au tain déchiré,
Redéfaire lointaine le vêtement
Rouge de ces années quand, infinie
Comme l'étoile aux vitres, tu prenais

Like too much sky. We worked here or there
In the vast rooms, spoke little, in rusty voices,
As if we were hiding a key under a stone.
Night sometimes came, from the edge of the fields,
A perfect dark bent woman driving her mute
Beasts through the waters of the constant sun.

And may she sleep
In the absolute that we have been,
This house that was like a ravine where the sky
Murmurs, where the dreaming bird comes to drink
The nocturnal stillness . . . Unrevealed,
Too vast, too mysterious for our steps,
Let us only brush her dark shoulder
And not disturb her who draws with calm breath
From the earth's reserves of dream. Night come,
Let us set down, simply, these stones
Where we read the sign, by her barren side.

What endless tasks we attempted,
What impenetrable signs we touched
With our ignorant, and therefore cruel, fingers!
What wrong ways, and what solitude!
Memory is weary, certainly, time narrow,
The path still infinite . . . But the sky
Has stones that glow more brightly on the slope
Of evening, and at this stop in our lives, light
Who sometimes increase, you catch and burn.

. . . .

Yes, by the night
High in our summer room
That goes like a ship, faltering at times
In the sky's foam (and I see you
Still, in the mirror whose silvering was torn,
Far away, undoing again the red
Gown of those years when, infinite
As the star in the windows, you took in your hands

A main de rêve inachevé dans les remous
Où déjà germe l'aube, du sommeil
La rose de chaque jour sinon mortelle.

Je regardais
Paraître l'autre barque, un feu
Lui aussi hésitant
Et lui aussi intact, comme la vie,
Dans les sarments de la montagne de Vachères.

Et je peux bien descendre
Encore, traverser les salles sombres,
Ouvrir, comme autrefois, faire ces pas
De chaque jour nouveau parmi les vignes
Dans l'immobilité à jamais du ciel,

Il fait beau,
La maison a duré comme l'étoile
Continue à monter dans le ciel clair,

Et la fille de Pharaon dort bien ici,
Les seins libres,
Sur cette couche que guide
Le courant du milieu du fleuve).

. . . .

Oui, par le « grand grenier »

Et Jean Aubry, d'Orgon,
Et ses fils Claude et Jean.
« Nous avons fait ce jour
Appui de communion. » La date manque.

Which were like an unfinished dream in the surf
Of sleep, when dawn already breaks,
The otherwise mortal rose of each day.

I watched
The other boat come in sight, it too
A hesitant fire,
It too intact, like life,
In the vine-shoots on the mountain of Vachères.

And I can still go down
The stairs, pass through the dim rooms,
Open the door, as before, take those first steps
Of each day among the vines
In the ever-stillness of the sky,

The day is fine,
The house has endured as the star
Goes on rising in the clear sky,

And indeed Pharaoh's daughter sleeps here,
Her breasts free,
On this couch guided
By the current in mid-river).

. . . .

Yes, by the "great loft"

And Jean Aubry, of Orgon,
And his sons Claude and Jean.
"This day we have installed
An altar rail." No date.

. . . .

Oui, par l'arche brisée
Du seuil
Dont nous avions trouvé la pierre manquante
—Passe, fleuve de paix, fais refleurir
L'œillet de cette rive.

. . . .

Oui, par la vitre brillante
Où, reformée,
La main de dehors simple tend le fruit
(Et cette barque est rouge, crépusculaire,
On dirait que le fruit du premier arbre
A terminé sa journée dans les branches
De la douleur du monde. Et il s'en va
Méditativement vers une autre rive.)

Oui, par ce feu,
Par son reflet de feu sur l'eau paisible,
Par notre lieu, qui va,
Par le chemin de feu sous le fruit mûr.

. . . .

Oui, par l'après-midi
Où tout est silencieux, étant sans fin,
Le temps dort dans la cendre du feu d'hier
Et la guêpe qui heurte à la vitre a cousu
Beaucoup déjà de la déchirure du monde.
Nous dormons, dans la salle d'en haut, mais nous allons
Aussi, et à jamais, parmi les pierres.

. . . .

Yes, by the broken arch
Of the threshold
Whose missing stone we had found
—Flow, river of peace, make
The carnation of this shore flower again.

. . . .

Yes, by the bright windowpane
Where, reformed,
The simple hand from outside offers the fruit
(And this boat is red, crepuscular,
You might think that the fruit of the first tree
Had ended its stay in the branches
Of the world's sorrow. That it moves
Thoughtfully toward another shore).

Yes, by this fire,
By its flame reflected in the still water,
By our place, which goes,
By the fire's path under the ripe fruit.

. . . .

Yes, by the afternoon
When all is silent, being without end,
Time sleeps in the ashes of yesterday's fire
And the wasp beating at the windowpane
Has already stitched up much of the world's tornness.
We sleep, in the upstairs room, but we also
Go, forever, among the stones.

. . . .

Oui, par le corps
Dans la douceur qui est aveugle et ne veut rien
Mais parachève.

Et à ses vitres les feuillages sont plus proches
Dans des arbres plus clairs. Et reposent les fruits
Sous l'arche du miroir. Et le soleil
Est haut encore, derrière la corbeille
De l'été sur la table et des quelques fleurs.

. . . .

Oui, par naître qui fit
De rien la flamme,
Et confond apaisés
Nos deux visages.

(Nous nous penchions, et l'eau
Coulait rapide,
Mais nos mains, là brisées,
Prirent l'image.)

. . . .

Oui, par l'enfant

Et par ces quelques mots que j'ai sauvés
Pour une bouche enfante. « Vois, le serpent
Du fond de ce jardin ne quitte guère
L'ombre fade du buis. Tous ses désirs
Sont de silence et de sommeil parmi les pierres.
La douleur de nommer parmi les choses
Finira. » C'est déjà musique dans l'épaule,
Musique dans le bras qui la protège,
Parole sur des lèvres réconciliées.

. . . .

Yes, by the body
In the easefulness that is blind and wants nothing
And yet perfects.

And at its windows the leaves are closer
In the brighter trees. And the fruit rests
Under the mirror's arch. And the sun
Is still high, behind the basket
Of a few summer flowers here, on the table.

. . . .

Yes, by birth
Which made the flame
Out of nothing, and mingles
Our two calmed faces.

(We bent down, and the water
Was flowing quickly,
But our hands, broken there,
Grasped the image.)

. . . .

Yes, by the child

And by these few words I've saved
For a child's mouth. "See, the snake
Down in the garden never leaves
The thin shade of the bush. He wants only
Silence and sleep among the stones.
The grief of giving names among things
Will end." It is already music in the shoulder,
Music in the sheltering arm around it,
Speech on reconciled lips.

. . . .

Oui, par les mots,
Quelques mots.

(Et d'une main,
Certes, lever le fouet, injurier le sens,
Précipiter
Tout le charroi d'images dans les pierres
—De l'autre, plus profonde, retenir.

Car celui qui ne sait
Le droit d'un rêve simple qui demande
A relever le sens, à apaiser
Le visage sanglant, à colorer
La parole blessée d'une lumière,
Celui-là, serait-il
Presque un dieu à créer presque une terre,
Manque de compassion, n'accède pas
Au vrai, qui n'est qu'une confiance, ne sent pas
Dans son désir crispé sur sa différence
La dérive majeure de la nuée.
Il veut bâtir! Ne serait-ce, exténuée,
Qu'une trace de foudre, pour préserver
Dans l'orgueil le néant de quelque forme,
Et c'est rêver, cela encore, mais sans bonheur,
Sans avoir su atteindre à la terre brève.

Non, ne démembre pas
Mais délivre, et rassure. « Écrire », une violence
Mais pour la paix qui a saveur d'eau pure.
Que la beauté,
Car ce mot a un sens, malgré la mort,
Fasse œuvre de rassemblement de nos montagnes
Pour l'eau d'été, étroite,

Et l'appelle dans l'herbe,
Prenne la main de l'eau à travers les routes,
Conduise l'eau d'ici, minime, au fleuve clair.)

. . . .

Yes, by the words,
A few words.

(And with one hand
Certainly, to raise the whip, curse at meaning,
And drive the whole load
Of images headlong into the stones
—But with the other, more profound, to hold back.

For he who does not know
The right of the simple dream, which wants
To watch over meaning, to calm
Its bloodied face, to bring
Color and light to the wounded word,
He, though he were
All but a god creating all but a world,
Is without compassion, does not arrive
At the truth, which is only trust, does not feel
In his craving clenched around his own difference
The main drift of the cloud.
He wants to build! Be it only, exhausted,
A stroke of lightning, to preserve
In pride the nullity of some form,
And that, too, is a dream, but luckless,
Unable to reach the brief earth.

No, do not dismember,
But deliver, and strengthen. "Writing," a violence
But for the sake of peace that tastes of pure water.
May beauty,
For this word has a meaning, in spite of death,
Do its work of gathering up our mountains
For summer's narrow water

And call it through the grass,
Take its hand along the way,
Lead the streams down from here to the clear river.)

. . . .

Oui, par la main que je prends
Sur cette terre.

Et dehors
C'est l'éclair à nouveau,
Se détachant,
Criant par-dessous, glissant,
Décolorant
La fin du ciel dans les pierres.

Passant à gué
Le peu profond ruisseau parmi les pierres.

. . . .

Oui, par la beauté, nue,
Avec du déchiré, du forclos dans le mouvement de l'épaule.

Oui, par toi—arrêtée
Au gué du ciel,
Foudre, robe entrouverte
Sur l'abondance de la terre aux fruits obscurs.

. . . .

Oui, par la mort,
Oui, par la vie sans fin.

. . . .

Par hier réincarné, ce soir, demain,
Oui, ici, là, ailleurs, ici, là-bas encore

. . . .

Yes, by the hand I take
On this earth.

And outside
There is lightning again,
Breaking loose,
Crying out from below, sliding,
Blanching
The end of the sky in the stones.

Fording
The shallow stream among the stones.

. . . .

Yes, by all beauty, naked,
With something torn, foreclosed in the movement of its shoulder.

Yes, by you—stopped
Midstream in the sky,
Lightning, dress slightly parted
Over the earth's abundance of dark fruits.

. . . .

Yes, by death,
Yes, by life without end.

. . . .

By yesterday reincarnated, by tonight, tomorrow,
Yes, here, there, elsewhere, here, over there again

(Et du livre rêvé, le feu
A tourné les pages.
Il les prit à la nuque et les alourdit
De sa morsure.
Elles ont disparu, selon
Son axe courbe
Qui les arqua, ainsi
Le mystère d'amour.)

. . . .

Oui, par même l'erreur,
Qui va,

Oui, par le bonheur simple, la voix brisée.

. . . .
. . . .

S'enfle (oui rassemblé, brûlé,
Dispersé,

Sel
Des orages qui montent, des éclaircies,
Cendre
Des mondes imaginaires dissipés,

Aube, pourtant,
Où des mondes s'attardent près des cimes.
Ils respirent, pressés
L'un contre l'autre, ainsi
Des bêtes silencieuses.
Ils bougent, dans le froid.
La terre est comme un feu de branches mouillées,
Le feu, comme une terre aperçue en rêve),

(And fire has turned the pages
Of the dreamt book.
Fire takes them by the neck and weights them
With its bite.
They have disappeared, lying back
Along the curved axis
Which bent them,
As the body is bent
In the mystery of love).

. . . .

Yes, by error even,
Which goes,

Yes, by humble happiness, by the broken voice.

. . . .
. . . .

Swells (yes gathered, burnt,
Scattered,

Salt
Of mounting storms, of clearings,
Ash
Of imaginary worlds dispelled,

Dawn, even so,
Where worlds linger near the summits,
Breathing, huddled
Against each other
Like silent beasts,
Stirring, in the cold.
The earth is like a fire of damp sticks,
The fire, like a land seen in dream),

Et brûle, oui, blanchisse puis déferle
(Vivre, nuées
Poussées mystérieusement, étinceler,
Finir,
Aile de l'impossible reployée)
La vague sans limite sans réserve.

. . . .

Les mots comme le ciel
Aujourd'hui,
Quelque chose qui s'assemble, qui se disperse.

Les mots comme le ciel,
Infini
Mais tout entier soudain dans la flaque brève.

And burns, yes, whitens and breaks
(Live, clouds
Mysteriously moved, flash
And end, wing
Of the impossible, folded back again)
The unlimited, unstinting wave.

. . . .

Words like the sky
Today,
Something that gathers, and scatters.

Words like the sky,
Infinite
But all here suddenly in the brief pool.

POETRY
BETWEEN
TWO WORLDS

Jean Starobinski

Poetry Between Two Worlds

They looked as they had heard of a world ransomed, or one destroyed.
This line from the last act of *The Winter's Tale*, the recognition scene
(V, 2), appears as an epigraph to Yves Bonnefoy's *Dans le leurre du
Seuil*.

The preceding volume, *Pierre écrite*, already had an epigraph from
the same play (III, 3): *Thou mettest with things dying: I with things
new-born.* Taken from a work Bonnefoy has translated admirably, and
whose mythical substance is dear to him, these epigraphs do not merely
imply the choice of a landmark in the great tradition of Western poetry;
they are the voice of the past alerting us and pointing to what is at
stake for us now; they indicate precisely, it seems to me, in an emble-
matic and seminal way, the double question that predominates in the
poetry of Yves Bonnefoy. The word "world" tells us that it has to do
with the world, or with *a* world; that is, with a coherent totality, and
a set of *real* relations. But the very existence of this world is in sus-
pense, in the alternation that opposes *ransomed* and *destroyed, things
dying* and *things new-born.* The poetic work here points to its initial
concern, the place it has sprung from: the moment of peril, where all
hovers between life and death, between "redemption" and "perdition."
The Shakespearean epigraphs, by the very force of their antitheses,
speak of tornness, of uncertainty, but also of the élan of hope: the
only sources—beyond any possessed assurance—that Bonnefoy assigns
to his poetry. They are its *constants.* The epigraph borrowed from
Hegel, at the head of Bonnefoy's first book, *Du movement et de
l'immobilité de Douve* (1953), already evokes the confrontation of life

and death: "But the life of the spirit is not frightened at death and does not keep itself pure of it. It endures death and maintains itself in it." The question of the *world*, in turn, was already pointed to, but critically, in the epigraph to the second book, *Hier régnant désert*, in a phrase taken from Hölderlin's *Hyperion*: "You want a world, said Diotima. That is why you have everything and yet have nothing." Here too the notion of the "world" is tied to an alternation, established in the great opposition of "all" and "nothing." For an artist so given to lucidity, the choice of epigraphs equals a declaration of intention, a guide to reading and comprehension, allowing us to see the new work in the light of past works, whose memory it has kept and to which it feels a need to respond. *The Winter's Tale* is a great myth of reconciliation. Behind the quotations from Hegel and Hölderlin we can discern the Neoplatonic themes of the One, of division, and of reintegration—questions whose urgency is renewed for Bonnefoy, beyond any guarantee assured by earlier art and thought. The passages he uses as epigraphs, words from the past, are an encouragement to consider the *present* situation of language as a moment when the human relation must be reborn, out of a state of dispersal. The quotation is a viaticum on the threshold of a journey that faces unexplored lands, the space of night, the places of disunion.

The *world* is in question: let us bear that in mind. And it is important for us to recall that the word *world*, especially in poetry, has acquired over the past two centuries a value that it did not have before. Earlier, it meant first the whole of creation within the order of nature; then, in the religious sense, it meant "this" world as opposed to "the other"; finally, in a looser sense, it signified a wide earthly space, a continent, "new" or "old." When Shakespeare speaks of a world "ransomed" or "destroyed," he takes the word in its religious sense, and, secondarily, in the last sense mentioned above, as a continent. But as we know, Shakespeare, a well as Montaigne, was witness to a crisis in the representation of the cosmos. Soon the Copernican image of the central sun, mathematical physics, calculative abstraction, reinforced by disciplined experience, would triumph. This new figure of the universe was constructed and described at the cost of a refusal of sensible appearances. The testimony of the senses gave credit to a world of substantial qualities; this was now called into doubt; henceforth it is only to the "inspection of the mind" (Descartes) that the secrets of nature will reveal themselves. The heavenly bodies, the *usable* forces of this earth, obey laws conforming to the rules of numbers, and can thus be anticipated and controlled. And if the evidence of the senses was required for the experiment, it was at the cost of abandoning the primary ground of sensible life. The development of mathematical physics, extended by that of technology, has generally increased the material security of mankind, and usurped the place of knowledge: these developments have put the *forces* of nature at the service of mankind (of human desires, in "this world"), but for the sake of that have had to renounce the contemplation of natural objects, of singular things—thus leaving unclaimed the entire realm in which what surrounds us is perceived in its color, its music, its palpable consistency. Joachim Ritter has shown that the *aesthetic* attention paid to landscape, in the West at least, arose at the moment when certain men sensed what they were in danger of losing by renouncing the wealth of spontaneous perception.[1] But he has insisted equally on the fact that landscape could be perceived as an object of disinterested pleasure only when scientific techniques had allowed men to feel less threatened by nature, less bound to the tasks of mere subsistence. Art and poetry thus receive as their share this realm abandoned by calculating reason, disqualified in the eyes of science, which constructs its systems from algebraic relations: the task of art henceforth is to repopulate it, to release its virtualities for happiness, even to pursue there a certain kind of knowledge, based on different proofs, and arising from a different legitimacy. Scientific knowledge "is informed by isolated systems" (to quote Bachelard), and remains scientific only insofar as it acknowledges its dependence on its choice of parameters; on the other hand, aesthetic activity takes up again the ancient function of *theoria tou cosmou*, the contemplation of the world as a totality and a meaning. Poetry, assuming responsibility for the world of appearances, does not limit itself to collecting the inheritance of the sensible world that scientific thought has turned away from. The triumph of physics and mathematical cosmology has brought with it the disappearance of religious representations tied to the ancient image of the cosmos: there no longer is any empyrean, any dwelling place of the angels or of God, beyond the planetary orbits. Nothing in the universe is different from this world; the profane world is the sole beneficiary of the application of scientific rationality. The sacred, if it is not to disappear, must take refuge in "inner" experience, join with the act of living, with communication, with shared love—and thus make its dwelling place the sensible, language, art.

This, it seems to me, is the paradoxical condition in which poetry has found itself, for not quite the past two centuries: a precarious condition, since it disposes of no such system of proofs as lends authority to scientific discourse, but at the same time a privileged condition in which poetry consciously assumes an ontological function —by which I mean at once an experience of being and a reflection on being—for which it did not have to bear the responsibility or the care in earlier centuries. Behind it there is a lost world, an order in which it was included, and which it knows cannot be revived. It carries within it the hope of a new order, a new meaning, whose establishment it must imagine. It brings everything to bear on the task of hastening the coming of the as yet unexpressed *world*, which is the ensemble of living relations in which we would find the fullness of a new presence. The world that poetry thus takes responsibility for is thought of as future, as the recompense for poetic labor. Rimbaud—one of those who has contributed most to imposing this new meaning on the word *world*—observes: "We are not in the world," and invokes: "O world! and the bright song of *new* sorrows."[2] An analogous space is designated as the *Weltinnenraum* towards which Rilke turned his thought (with the most sensitive expectation).

The work of Bonnefoy offers us today one of the most committed and deeply pondered examples of this modern vocation of poetry. His writings as poet and essayist, in which the personal accent is so clear, and in which the *I* of subjective assertion is manifested with force and simplicity, have for object a relation to the world, not an internal reflection on the self.[3] This *oeuvre* is one of the least narcissistic there is. It is entirely turned toward the external object which is what matters for it, and whose singularity, whose unique character, always implies the possibility of sharing. Subjective assertion is thus only the first term of a relation whose developed form is the summons: the *you* that is addressed to another person (to reality outside the self), but equally the *you* in which the poet transcribes an appeal addressed to him, are at least as insistent as the *I* of personal affirmation. The self, one might say, is kept alert by its care for the world, to which it is accountable through its use of language. Turning to the vocabulary of ethics, Bonnefoy tells us that what is at stake is a common *good*— a *good* which must necessarily be realized and felt in individual experience, but not solely for the benefit of the separate individual. The subject, the self, so forcefully present in the act of expression, does not remain alone on stage in what it expresses: it leaves much room for the other, for what demands compassion, and accepts that individual consciousness, in the face of the world, must bend to the demands of a *truth* which it has no right to dispose of arbitrarily. The solipsism of much "poetic discourse" in the modern age draws the strongest objections from Bonnefoy. It is not the self but the world that must be "ransomed," or more precisely: the self cannot be "ransomed" unless the world is "ransomed" with it. About this point, too, the epigraph is entirely revealing.

Having studied mathematics, logic and the history of science as a young man, Bonnefoy knows by experience the attraction of abstract thought, the joy the mind can take in building a structure of pure concepts and relations. But like Bachelard, whose courses in science he attended, he knows that precision of knowledge demands the sacrifice of immediate details, of primary images—and this he cannot accept. Bachelard, too, after having exalted scientific asceticism, was taken with what he himself had rejected: the convictions of dreams, the configuration that desire gives to space, the imaginary virtues we attribute to matter. But for Bonnefoy, who differs here from Bachelard, it is not an imaginary dimension that is needed to safeguard the fire necessary for life, but a *reality*, simple, full, meaning-bearing—an earth, as he will insist. Not that imagination and dream have not exerted a persistent seduction on Bonnefoy's mind: the few years when he sympathized with surrealism attest to that. But he soon felt that what revealed itself in the "marvels" of surrealism was not the "background of sensible experience, with riches unknown to ordinary reason, but an *evil presence* in which what-is withdraws itself in the same moment that it appears to our eyes, and closes itself to our reading. . . ."[4] Rereading this text in which Bonnefoy explains his break with the surrealists, we see clearly what, in his view, should prevail against the *image*, which shines with "the idea of a different light:" it is "reality" ("which is more than surreal"), it is "simple things," "the figure of our place," it is finally the "world:"

> (. . .) There is true presence only when sympathy, which is the act of consciousness, can pass like a thread not only through certain aspects which lend themselves to reveries but through *all dimensions of the object, the world,* taking them up, reintegrating them in a unity which I for my part feel is guaranteed us by the earth, in its obviousness, the earth which is life.[5]

The reproach Bonnefoy addresses to surrealism, symmetrically inverse to that which he addresses to science, is of having abandoned the place, the world allotted to us, in the name of a *different* order of reality, which reveals itself only in a fugitive way, to privileged beings at privileged moments; the *aura* which such a person or object suddenly takes on—in surrealist experience—has the effect of persuading us "that a part of our reality, this object, bears . . . within itself the traces, at the very least, of a superior reality, which devalues, in return, *the other things of the world*, and gives us the feeling that the *earth is a prison. . . .*"[6] That, for Bonnefoy, is the sign of a gnostic attitude: an attitude which, to justify its rejection of the appearances of the world, appeals to the notion of a lost unity, of a fall, of the necessary quest for salvation in another region of reality. The presence *of* the world, and our presence *in* the world, which Bonnefoy feels so intense a need for, must, it seems to him, be maintained against all dreams and against all appeals that draw our spirit toward separate realms. Surrealism, yielding to the attractions of astrology and occultism (whose ascendency dominates the postwar writings of André Breton), simply offers a prescientific version, a "magical" version, of the discourse of deterministic science: its quest for the secret alienates it no less from the immediate, from the "simple," from concrete existence, and in that sense is no less dissociating than the law of concepts and numbers.

We should note here that the *world* whose emergence Bonnefoy seeks to assure takes its full meaning only from the opposition it maintains: it is the world won back from abstraction, the world freed from the nocturnal waters of dream; and this implies effort, work, journey. The world, even if we finally come to realize that it was *already there*, is at first absent, veiled, and must be recovered, by the eye and the word, from a situation of isolation and want. All of Bonnefoy's texts— poetry, prose, essays—include a sequence of moments, comparable to moments of passage, in which a desire keeps watch divided between memory and hope, between nocturnal cold and the warmth of a new fire, between denunciation of the "lure" and straightness of sight. They are situated, so to speak, between two worlds (in personal history as well as in collective history): there *was* a world, a fullness of meaning, but they have been lost, broken, scattered. (This affirmation is the starting point of gnostic doctrines—and the fact that he shares it with them makes Bonnefoy all the more careful to separate himself from them later on.) For him who does not let himself be taken in by chimeras, or by despair, there *will be* a world once more, a habitable place; and this place is not "elsewhere," or "yonder," it is "here"—in the place itself, found again like a new shore, in a new light. But this new shore is only foreshadowed, prefigured, discovered by hope. So that this space *between two worlds* may be considered the field in which Bonnefoy's work develops—a field necessarily open to images of movement and journeying, which sometimes calls for narration, with all the "adventures" that take place in stories of quest: wanderings, traps, false paths, the entering of ports and gardens. In fact, this spatial projection is only an image, an allegorical virtuality which Bonnefoy knows he must also defend himself against. Between two worlds: the trajectory is essentially one of life and thought, it is constituted by the change of relations with objects and beings, by the development of an experience of language.

Bonnefoy's extreme exactingness with regard to the *authenticity* of the second world he wishes to come to determines a series of warnings or means of nonacceptance with regard to what threatens to turn him from it or to take the place of it too completely. We must go so far as to say that, precisely because of its projection into the future, beyond the point reached by our investigation, the second world is defined less by its own character (which can be revealed only by its advent) than by the rejection of illusory or partial worlds that offer themselves in its place.

This dimension of future and hope is essential. However intense his feeling of a lost world, Bonnefoy does not let the backward glance or nostalgic thought prevail. Often, of course, he lets it be known that in the past of human cultures there was a sacred alliance with the earth, testimony of which has been gathered by the mythologies: but mythical utterance has ceased, and cannot be reborn in its old form. It only indicates the possibility of a fullness that human existence was capable of in a world prior to the schism that separated the language of science (of the concept) from that of poetry. Henceforth it is the task of poetry, or at least of a new practice of the word, to invent a new relation to the world—a relation which, charged with *memory* though it may be, will not be a *repetition* of the old alliance. If we glimpse fleetingly, in Bonnefoy, the light of a former unity, it never yields to restorative (or regressive) reveries, which would make do with a simulacrum of return: Bonnefoy limits himself to evoking, forcefully but without insistence, a first intimacy with natural innocence. For the break, or "fall," is too obvious to him for him to engage in any act of pure restoration: reveries of a golden age, the lyricism of the idyll, are foreign to him. Such a "fixation of regret" is imaginable only for someone who hopes to avoid difficult confrontations, who can be content with an "image" in place of the missing "reality." No worship of the past, then, even though a certain past, difficult to pinpoint, appears privileged in relation to our present condition. The first world can no longer serve as our refuge. If Bonnefoy, in his essays, happens to use words, mainly verbs, marked by the prefix of repetition —to "reanimate" or "recenter" speech, to "recommence a dwelling place," to "recover presence"—we should know that he is not inviting the return of a former fullness, or attributing an unsurpassable authority to it: it is a matter of defining the second world as the place of a new life, another fullness, a different unity, through which the loss of the first world may in some sense be made good. Keeping his distance with regard to Christianity and Hegel, Bonnefoy remains attached nonetheless to a certain figure of progression, of the step forward, which hopes to find *in the end*, in a simplified and more intimately possessed truth, thanks to the work of mediation (which is trial and death), that which was lost or abandoned *in the beginning*. The backward look is certainly not impugned: poetic works, languages, myths call for hearing and meditation, but in order to nourish hope and to turn the mind toward what is still unknown.

To entrust the task to language, to poetry, is, for Bonnefoy, to posit in principle that the second world has its basis in the act of speech which names things and calls them into "being" in a living communication with the other person (our neighbor). In his texts on art and poetry, Bonnefoy defines this task mainly by way of negation, by exposing the peril attaching to the use of language, when it breaks with the world, and above all with the other person, and opts proudly for its own autonomous perfection. He often returns to this point, and his commentators, beginning with Maurice Blanchot, have paid sufficient attention to it, so that we need not set out here all the arguments with which Bonnefoy arms his warning against the seductions that would turn us from the quest for the "true place" and "entrap" us (the word expresses very well a final ill-fated immobilization) in a separate universe. This warning is not only theoretical; it is not only an article of aesthetic or anti-aesthetic doctrine promoting some sort of "death of art" as a condition of access to the second world. Reading *L'Arrière-pays* ["The Back-Country"], which testifies to Bonnefoy's personal development, we observe that for him it is a question of a peril intimately experienced in the gnostic temptation of an "elsewhere," in the fever induced by the call, "yonder," of a "true place" which is only the illusion of the true place, since it demands a desertion of the *here and now*, of the reality in which the poet finds himself uncentered, exiled. Separation is a sin: it is the sin committed by "speakers of words"[7] when they abandon the "real" (or being) for their own notions; when the dream turns to the distance; when the image, in its glory, prevails over the humble presence of things; when the book or work isolates itself in its closed perfection, aloof, in the "abstract" purity of its structure. There is a deadly power in language —when it supplants reality by concealing it, by replacing it with an image, an insubstantial reflection. It must then be reduced to silence. But nothing can alter the fact that language is also the bearer of our "hope of presence." Thus the peril of the choice between a "world destroyed" or a "world ransomed" is lodged in writing itself. If there is somewhere a danger that threatens "being," Bonnefoy does not claim to be untouched by it, or lay the blame for it only on some evil force outside himself: the age, society, deceitful ideologies. He admits to seeing it in the signs his own hand traces, in objects whose beauty holds his attention, in the false "gnostic" way on which his own dream of salvation risks losing itself. There exists, then, for Bonnefoy, not only a first schism (for which, as we have seen, the "concept" bears its share of responsibility), but an increased loss in addition, when deliverance is sought in an "image-world," through what Bonnefoy again calls a "concept," but this time referring to purified words, verbal essences, dreamed forms. The image-world is the product of an aggravated sin, even if we must recognize at its source a genuine hope of unity, an impulse toward fullness: for the impulse becomes fixed in a "mask," and creates an obstacle that comes between our desire and its finality—real presence. Of course the image world, the mask-world, is the negation of the impoverished and "disassembled" world in which we live in a state of waiting; but these words, these essences, which are born of a sacrifice of the immediate, of a putting to death of the first principle of existence, do not give birth and life to the second world: they shine with the brightness of death. The exigency of which Bonnefoy makes himself the spokesman (an ethical, or rather an ontological exigency, far more than an aesthetic one) calls for a second negation, a second death, a negation of the negation: an "existential" negation of the "intellectual" negation which produced the work: the closed figure in which "Beauty" is isolated, the system (the verbal world) in which *language* or, better, the *work* as language, is imprisoned, must be broken, consumed, abused, shattered, so that out of this enduring of death *speech* may be born, the living act of communication. Let us immediately add one observation on this point: it is because conceptual organisms in their expansive pride, in their "cold" radiance and in their power of concealment take on the figure of the world, that this word is most often replaced by others when it is a question of designating what we have called the "second world:"

Bonnefoy speaks more readily of a *second earth* (the title of an essay from *Le Nuage rouge* ["The Red Cloud"]), or *land*; he also speaks of a *true place*. For the word *world*, heavy with reminiscences from antiquity, when the stable character of *harmony* was attributed to the cosmos, does not say enough about finitude, mortality, time granted in passing moments, which are the lot of earthly life, to which we are asked to assent. And we see Bonnefoy regularly turning to the word *world* to denounce the *intelligible* worlds, or *languages*,[8] enclosed in their own perfection.

The earth recovered, thanks to a living speech that would be able to reunite, to *reassemble*. This word, often used by Bonnefoy in his essays, and which appears at the end of *Dans le leurre du seuil*, belongs to that category we have already mentioned of words with the prefix of repetition, but meaning more than a simple return. To reassemble (conjugated most often in the conditional, the mode of a hope that clings to no certainty), is to realize the "co-presence" which the concept had promised but never truly achieved. It announced a simultaneous grasp: *con-cipere*, *be-greifen*—their etymological kinship makes them near equivalents of *reassemble*. But, if we listen to Bonnefoy, the concept universalizes thought about the object, but misses the object itself in its finite presence. The pride of this mental *grasp* avoids the pain of incarnation: using an emphatic term, Bonnefoy speaks in this connection of *excarnation*. On the contrary, to reassemble, as Bonnefoy defines it in some of his most striking texts, is to hold precarious existences together, in the light of the moment, sustained by meaning, attaining to being by grace of a speech that has opened itself to them, preferring them to itself, in trust and compassion.

The earth, the place, the simple, have no need, then, to lay an entire world out before us: it is enough if the few needful precursory words announce it, bringing proof of its truth. The "second earth" is not to be reached through a proliferation of tangible species, in the bad infinity of the enumeration of things (unless, as in one of the qualities Bonnefoy admires in Saint-John Perse, each word, charged with memory of the real, can awaken those momentary divinities previously encountered in childhood, at the heart of the natural world). His fundamental intuition does not lead him to verbal luxuriance, great lexical floods, the polyphony of perceptions—even though he attributes to regenerated language the uplifting power of a wave (the "tide that uplifts,"[9] the "unlimited, unstinting wave"[10]). The ark he builds is not one of exhaustiveness. Only those words should come to life in poetry which have, in the poet's conscience, gone through the test of meaning, which have been torn from coldness and inertia to be joined by a living bond. For Bonnefoy it is not the multiplicity of things named that matters, but the quality of the relation that brings them into reciprocal presence—a relation one might have called syntactical, if syntax did not exhaust itself in the order it sets up: it is a question, in Bonnefoy's hope, of a movement that establishes (or re-establishes) an order, which comes through and *opens*—the metaphor of opening is a suitable one for reconciling fidelity (the *recovery* of the world, or at least the *recalling* of it) and the inaugural function that devolves upon speech (beginning to live according to meaning). The ambition expressed many times by Bonnefoy is to "clarify" a few of the words "that help us live." An apparently limited pledge, but one that takes on a conquering élan in the image of dawn ("this gleam that appears in the east, out of densest night") or of a fire catching and beginning to glow. The task assigned to poetry is that of making "a' few great reanimated words live together, opening on an infinite radiance."[11] The infinity is in the radiance, not in the multiplicity of words. Or, as a more recent text says:

> Let us stop "abolishing" chance, as words enable us to do. On the contrary, let us take it upon ourselves. Then the presence of the other, to which we sacrifice the infinite, and consequently our own presence to ourselves, will open a possibility for us. Certain events, those that mark out a destiny, will separate themselves, as significant, from the field of mute appearances. Certain words— bread and wine, house, even storm or stone—will likewise detach themselves, as words of communion, of meaning, from the web of concepts. And a place will begin to take shape from these assumptions and symbols, which, though certainly nothing in its ultimate substance, will be our completed human form, and hence unity in action and the advent of being in its own absoluteness. Incarnation, which is beyond dreams, is a proximate good.[12]

Other texts, similarly oriented, introduce considerations aimed at attenuating the aspect of parousia or utopia which, however, can never be completely separated from the advent of the "second earth." At least they insist on the idea that it can never be attained once and for all. And they affirm the central responsibility of the subject (often raised to the collective: we) who makes the act of language:

. . . No, if one devotes oneself to words that say hearth, tree, road, wandering, return, it will not necessarily bring deliverance; even in a sacralized world the spirit of possession can come back to life, making presence once again into an object, and living knowledge once more into a science, suddenly impoverished: but at least he who wishes to may work without inner contradiction to *reassemble what greed has disassembled,* and then that *co-presence* may be reformed *in which the earth becomes speech,* and the heart will be appeased because it can hear it at last and even mix its voice with others. *The world of these words,* in effect, has no structure except through *us,* who have built it of the sand and lime from outside.[13]

The clarity of this conviction, documented in writings at once ardent and patient, has no need of external confirmation. Yet I cannot help mentioning here what I have read in one of the best philosophers of our time. At the end of his *Logique de la philosophie,* which extends and reinterprets Hegelian thought, Eric Weil introduces the category of *Meaning,* and insists on presence: "Poetry is the creator of concrete meaning. Where there is no such creation (which may be, and at certain moments of history can only be, creation *against* an existing meaning, destructive creation), there is no poetry, and there is poetry everywhere that a meaning appears, whatever its 'form' may be. . . . In this broadest and deepest sense . . . poetry is not the concern of gifted and talented men: it is the concern of man himself. . . . Poetry is presence. . . . It is immediate Unity, and the poet does not know . . . if he has spoken of himself or of the world."[14]

What is said here by a thinker much taken with conceptual precision is inscribed and fixed once and for all in a definitive formulation. Whereas, though their aims converge, what characterizes Bonnefoy's approach is the multiplicity of forms and metaphorical figures through which he evokes the possible advent of presence and unity. Considering only the essays and prose texts of Bonnefoy, we could cite a dozen more passages analogous to those that have been partially quoted already. Texts in which we of course find some of the same words, and the same use of the conditional mode of hope, but in which the rhythm, the system of images are renewed each time—to speak tirelessly of one and the same transfiguration, which is the illumination of the real, once all conceptual *forms* are set aside. Bonnefoy repeats the promise of this advent in ceaseless variations, as if to abolish the figure he had given it in the previous writing, and to prove its possibility by mobility, by infinite liberty, by the breaking down of limits. We see here the best evidence of a tenacious hope that seizes every chance to be explicit, with an élan that is never the same though always turned toward the same end. Incessant renewal in the expression of hope is required to the extent that "presence" aspires to free itself from a certain anguish, and to distinguish itself from all that is fixed in *writing*. For "presence" not to be concealed by the images that give name to it, or simply call on it, they must be fluid, impermanent, must be able, so to speak, to slip past each other, so that dwelling, earth, fire, the moment can exchange their symbolic power. This aspect of the essays and texts on art relates them very closely to Bonnefoy's poems themselves. The critical expression in these pages is in a relation of continuity with the voice that speaks in the poetic works. The poem constitutes a putting to the test of what, in the essay, is only pointed out from a distance: the common horizon, seen through the essays and poetry of Bonnefoy, is (to borrow a term he often uses) the same *moment*. Its approach is announced by an increased luminosity, by a sense of simplification and reconciliation—in a changed diction in which the accent of consent succeeds that of struggle, and at the same time, even in the syntax, the network of formal constraints opens out.

But the number of these leaps which, in Bonnefoy's essays, reach to the verge of presence finally held to be possible, calls for still more commentary: the leaps are so many because, once hope is expressed, one must come back to the world—or rather to the absence of world to which history has doomed us; one must come back to our time of wandering and waiting, to the space between two worlds. And start again from there. After having greeted the dawn, and even celebrated the new day, to come back to the gray and the cold—not without a certain knowledge, of course, not without an awareness of the traps to be avoided, of the illusions of desire.

And again the temptation of separate worlds, the appeal of images, the help demanded of writing and its captive forms arise. So that once again one finds it necessary to tear oneself away from this "image-world," to call down upon it the consuming "lightning"—that our eyes may be opened to the "true place." *Recommencement* has become an insistent motif in Bonnefoy's thought:

> A moment of true light on some stony road I am walking down one morning or evening will be quite enough to cast on the writing that glancing light which reveals its useless reliefs and empty holes. And this higher truth will help me then to correct my desire, to simplify it: leading of course to another dream in another piece of

writing—one cannot break the circle—but it will be at once more elementary and more encompassing, a place where the other will already be better received and finitude more fully understood. To write, of course—who can help it? But, also, through an experience complementary to the poem, through the maturation that the poem alone permits, to *unwrite* the fantasms and chimeras from the past which would otherwise darken our path. And henceforth, generally speaking, no book blindly confirmed two years later by another book, but a life in which, writing being no more even in the depth of its polysemous images than a scribbling that is gradually erased, what takes shape little by little, and will speak as such, is a presence in itself, a destiny: a finitude that grows bright and thus keeps watch over meaning. No, this book I have just written is nothing, precisely because it is all. The world that holds my attention at this step, is also the footprint one leaves behind, the pause that may again become an advance by a decision that comes from something other in us—the way, then, towards that invisibility ahead, which is the place.[15]

Recommencement is here assumed to be the very condition of progress. But two distinct times are affirmed and we are told that they must be repeated: the moment when hope is enclosed in the world of words it has made for itself, and the break "ahead" which sacrifices words for a future inhabited by more truth. To leave the arid world for "writing," then to leave writing (inevitably wrong) for the "place." This too can only be written, and escapes that peril only by being written again, in another way, in words felt to be less opaque. *Dans le leurre du seuil* begins at a moment of ebb: the reassembling (which already took place) is undone, meaning (which had shone) is scattered; we are back in the night again. To what has proved to be only a dream (which "failed of celebration"), a new dream succeeds. Negation appears once more, at the very beginning:

> But no, once again
> Unfolding the wing of the impossible
> You awaken, with a cry,
> From the place which is only a dream. . . .[16]

External reality is perceived once again not in its incarnate presence, in its finitude, but merely as the reflection of a world located elsewhere:

The field that seems painted on nothing,
The masses of light sandstone in the ravine,
Are barely trembling, perhaps the reflection
Of other trees and stones in a river.[17]

To claim that appearance is only a reflection, is, according to Bonne-foy, the eternal "platonising" temptation, which haunts Western thought. He recalls this in a recent study of the haiku, which offers the occasion of comparing two attitudes toward the real:

> I want to show the glittering white cloud in which everything is scattered and vanishes, and at that same moment, in thought, I'm in one of our villages in the mountains, with its heavy sandstone houses, a place unlike any in Japan, made for holding the absolute in our existence as a fire is preserved between the stones of a hearth: and I come out of one such house, half ruined but thereby alive, and see on the horizon at sunset a red cloud flaming the sky with its light, *of which I always ask myself if it is not the reflection of another*.[18]

In the future, too, the "leap toward the impossible" will be repeated, a recent text tells us, though at the end of *Dans le leurre du seuil*, answering the second verse of the long poem (in which the "wing of the impossible" is unfolded), unity is promised among things brought back to presence—the "wing of the impossible, *folded back again*."[19] The step is never taken for good. One must start again from the dream, and again repudiate it.

Repudiate it? Perhaps, finally, Bonnefoy (the author of admirable dream-stories) comes to something like an armed truce with it. Perhaps, without losing his hope of the "true place," he comes to accept that the space of the act of speech should be between two worlds, even in a double sense: between the arid world of our exile and the image-world constructed by words, and then between this mirage and the "garden of presence." Perhaps he must consent to the image, to form, to the structures of language (which are a conceptual exile), in order to accede to presence, which is not a second transcendence but a willing return to the precarious truth of appearances. The image may bring us there, despite its "coldness," if we avoid solidifying it, if we are able to make it admit its own precariousness. At the end of *Dans le leurre du seuil*, the worlds (image-worlds, as I read them) re-form again after being scattered:

Ash
Of imaginary worlds dispelled,

Dawn, even so,
Where worlds linger near the summits,
Breathing, huddled
Against each other
Like silent beasts,
Stirring, in the cold.[20]

The two times—of a refusal of the imaginary, then of a return to the imaginary, but pluralized, and "breathing" now—are marked here, to my mind, in the clearest way. It seems as if the imaginary, accused of having concealed reality, of having slandered appearances, of having set itself up as a separate world, is finally received as a legitimate part of a vaster, reconciled world. A text on Basho admirably indicates this same consent to what had been denounced as a concealing force (language as a stable structure, formal beauty), on condition that what produces the opening intervene immediately. Bonnefoy perceives the fine dividing line that marks, within a brief poem (a haiku), the divergence of two worlds:

> . . . Listening more intensely, you hear two sounds under this appearance of fixed stars, two sounds at once distinct and very close like the cry of the barn-owl, and this union within difference is itself the dialectic of wandering and return. . . . Notions, yes, at first, that structure which tends to exist as soon as there are words in our mouths, and the lightning exchanges between them in the realm of the intelligible. . . . The moment of excarnation, always virtual in language as its native failing, is succeeded by the cry of incarnation. Which is sometimes as slight as the falling of a dry leaf, but what more is needed than a few ripples on the water for the idea of the instant to trouble the peace of essence?[21]

The two times—and the divergence of two worlds—are here brought extremely close—initiating a "dialectic" held in a "brief duration." An attentive examination will show that this "dialectic" is at work every moment in the very issue of *Dans le leurre du seuil*, so that the between-two-worlds makes itself felt not only between the opening and the final lines of the poem, but everywhere, even in the closing verses:

Words like the sky
Today,
Something that gathers, and scatters.

Words like the sky,
Infinite
But all here suddenly in the brief pool.[22]

The *double* element is everywhere: the image-world of words and the open space of the sky; the time of gathering, immediately followed by scattering; infinity, but captured in the "brief pool" (reflection and image legitimized, by very reason of their precariousness, their brevity); space above, where clouds pass, and the earthly soil, where water lies humbly in the pool. . . . In these simple words the conflict is appeased, but the threshold has not been crossed: the peace that comes allows the divergence of the two worlds to remain, the opposition without which unity would have no meaning.

—JEAN STAROBINSKI

Endnotes

[1] Joachim Ritter, *Subjektivität*, Frankfort, 1974, pp. 141–190. The essay on landscape appeared in French in *Argile*, XVI, Paris, summer 1978, trans. Gérard Raulet.

[2] See the commentary on *"Génie"* in Bonnefoy's study, *Rimbaud*, Paris, 1961, pp. 147–148.

[3] Cf. John E. Jackson, *La Question du sujet. Un aspect de la modernité poétique européenne: T. S. Eliot, Paul Celan, Yves Bonnefoy*, Neuchâtel, La Baconnière, 1978.

[4] "Entretien avec John E. Jackson," *L'Arc*, 1976, No. 66, pp. 85–92.

[5] *Op. cit.*, p. 90.

[6] *Op. cit.*, p. 89.

[7] "The poet is a speaker of words," writes Pierre Jean Jouve, in *Tombeau de Baudelaire*. Bonnefoy's study of Jouve (in *Le Nuage rouge*) rejects the idea of salvation through poetry.

[8] *Le Nuage rouge*, 1977, p. 280.

[9] See p. 177 of this edition.

[10] *Poèmes*, p. 332.

[11] *Un rêve fait à Mantoue*, collected in *L'Improbable*, new edition, 1980, p. 66.

[12] *Le Nuage rouge*, pp. 278–279.

[13] *Le Nuage rouge*, pp. 342–343. Starobinski's emphasis.

[14] Eric Weil, *Logique de la philosophie*, Paris, 1950, pp. 421–422.

[15] *Le Nuage rouge*, p. 76.

[16] See p. 177 of this edition. On the wing that vibrates in the sky, and its value as a sign announcing a "yonder"—hence a "back-country"—see the essay on Morandi in *Le Nuage rouge*, p. 112.

¹⁷ See p. 63 of this edition.

¹⁸ Preface to *Haiku,* foreword and French text by Roger Munier, Paris, 1978, pp. xxxv–xxxvi.

¹⁹ See p. 177 of this edition.

²⁰ See p. 175 of this edition.

²¹ *Le Nuage rouge,* p. 344.

²² See p. 171 of this edition.

The interview with John E. Jackson quoted in the course of this preface has been collected in Yves Bonnefoy, *Entretiens sur la poésie,* La Baconnière, Neuchâtel, 1981.

About the Author

YVES BONNEFOY, who is widely recognized as one of France's leading poets, was born in Tours in 1923. His principal collections of poems are: *Du mouvement et de l'immobilité de Douve* (1953); *Hier régnant désert* (1958); *Pierre écrite* (1965); and *Dans le leurre du seuil* (1975). He has also published works of art and literary criticism, and translations of many of Shakespeare's plays. Since 1981, he has been professor at the Collège de France.

About the Translator

RICHARD PEVEAR is the author of two books of poems, *Night Talk* and *Exchanges*. He has also translated Alain's *The Gods* and Sophocles's *Ajax*. He lives in New York.